The Canadian's Guide to Modern Investing

by Tyler Bain, Brendan Bradley, Susanne Chishti, Kiana Danial, Steve Gormley, James Jockle, Peter Kent, Seoyoung Kim, Matt Krantz, Tiana Laurence, James Maendel, Paul Mladjenovic, Steven R. O'Hanlon, Dawn Patrick, and Russell Wild

WILEY

Publisher's Acknowledgments

Authors: Tyler Bain, Brendan Bradley, Susanne Chishti, Kiana Danial, Steve Gormley, James Jockle, Peter Kent, Seoyoung Kim, Matt Krantz, Tiana Laurence, James Maendel, Paul Mladenovic, Steven R. O'Hanlon, Dawn Patrick, and Russell Wild

Senior Acquisitions Editor: Tracy Boggier

Project Editor: Elizabeth Kuball

Compilation Editor: Georgette Beatty

Production Editor: Saikarthick Kumarasamy

Cover Photo: © serkorkin/Getty Images

The Canadian's Guide to Modern Investing

Published by John Wiley & Sons, Inc.
111 River St.
Hoboken, NJ 07030-5774
`http://www.wiley.com`

For general information on our other products and services, please contact our Business Development Department in the U.S. at 317-572-3205.

Library of Congress Control Number: 2022937977

ISBN 978-1-119-89631-9 (pbk)

SKY10041502_011923

Table of Contents

1

Get Yourself Ready

Before doing something risky, you probably think good and hard about what you stand to gain and what you might lose. Surprisingly, many investors, especially those just starting out, lose that innate sense of risk and reward. They chase the biggest possible returns without considering the sleepless nights they'll suffer through as those investments swing up and down. Some start buying investments they've heard that others made money on without thinking about whether those investments are appropriate for them. Worst of all, some fall prey to fraudsters who promise huge returns in get-rich-quick schemes.

So, we've decided to start from the top and make sure that the basics are covered. In this chapter, you discover tips for saving money to use for investing and get a grip on investing lingo. You also find out what kind of investor you are by using online tools that measure your taste for risk. After you've become familiar with your inner investor, you can start thinking about forming an investment plan that won't give you an ulcer.

It's only natural if you're feeling skittish when it comes to investing, especially if you're just starting out. After all, it has been a brutal couple of decades even for veteran investors. Some people think all the chaos is just too much to bear and choose to avoid stocks altogether. That decision is a mistake, though. Prudent investing can be a great way for you to reach your financial goals. You just need an approach that will maximize your returns while cutting your risks.

Turn Yourself into a Big Saver

Investing can help you accomplish some great things. It can help you pay for a child's college tuition, buy the house you've been eyeing, retire in style, or travel to the moon. Okay, maybe not the last one. But you get the idea. Investing helps your money grow faster than inflation. And by investing online, you can profit even more by reducing the commissions and fees you must pay to different advisors and brokers.

One thing online investing can't do is make something out of nothing. To make money investing online, you have to save money first. Don't get frustrated, though, because you don't need as much to get started as you might fear. If you have a job or source of income, building up ample seed money isn't too hard.

If you want to be an investor, you must find ways to spend less money now so that you can save the excess. That means you must retrain yourself from being a consumer to being an investor. Many beginning investors have trouble getting past this point because being a consumer is so easy. Consumers buy things that they can use and enjoy now, but almost all those objects lose value over time. Cars, electronic gadgets, and clothing are all examples of things consumers "invest" their money in. You don't even have to have money to spend — plenty of credit card companies will gladly loan it to you. Consumers fall into this spending pattern vortex and end up living paycheck to paycheck with nothing left to invest.

Investors, on the other hand, find ways to put off current consumption. Instead of spending money, they invest it into building businesses or goods and services that can earn money, rather than deplete it.

TIP

Here are a few things you can do now to help you change from being a consumer to being an investor:

- **Start with what you can manage by putting aside a little each month.**
- **Keep increasing what you put aside.** If you do it gradually, you won't feel the sting of a suddenly pinched pocket.
- **Hunt for deals and use coupons and discounts.** Put aside the saved money.
- **Buy only what you need.** Don't be fooled into buying things you don't need because they're on sale.

Decide How You Plan to Save

After you've determined how much you need to save and how much you can save, it's time to put your plan into action. The way you do this really depends on how good you are at handling your money and saving. The different methods are as follows:

- **Automatic withdrawals:** Ever heard the cliché "Pay yourself first"? It's a trite saying that actually makes sense. The idea is that before you go shopping for that big-screen TV or start feeling rich after payday, you should set aside money for savings. Some people have the discipline to do this themselves, but many do not. For the latter group of people, the best option is to set up *automatic withdrawals,* which are a way of giving a brokerage firm or bank permission to automatically extract money once a month. When the money is out of your hands, you won't be tempted to spend it.

- **Retirement plans:** If your goal is investing for retirement, you want to find out what retirement savings plans are available to you. When you're starting to invest, taking advantage of available retirement plans is usually your best bet.
- **On your own:** If you have money left over after paying all your bills, don't let it sit in a savings account. Leaving cash in a low-interest-bearing account is like giving a bank a cheap loan. Put your money to work for you. Brokers make it easy for you to get money to them via electronic transfers.

Learn the Lingo

Just about any profession, hobby, or pursuit has its own lingo. Car fanatics, chess players, and computer hobbyists have terms of art that they seem to learn through osmosis. Investing is no different. You might have heard but not completely understood many terms, such as *stocks* and *bonds.* As you read through this book and browse the websites we mention, you'll probably periodically stumble on unfamiliar words.

Don't expect a standard dictionary to help much. Investing terms can be so specialized and precise that your dusty ol' dictionary might not be a big help. Fortunately, a number of excellent online investing glossaries explain in detail what investing terms mean. Here are a couple for you to check out:

- **Investopedia** (`www.investopedia.com`) has one of the most comprehensive databases of investing terms, with thousands of entries. The site not only covers the basics but also explains advanced terms in great detail. It's also fully searchable so you won't waste time getting the answer.
- **Harvey's Hypertextual Finance Glossary** (`http://people.duke.edu/~charvey/Classes/wpg/glossary.htm`) is all about quick answers. The database, written by Campbell Harvey, a professor of finance at Duke University, explains most basic investment terms in one or two sentences.

Gut-Check Time: How Much Risk Can You Take?

It's time to get a grip — a grip on how much you can invest, that is. Most beginning investors are so interested in finding stocks that make them rich overnight that they lose sight of risk. But academic studies show that risk and return go hand in hand. That's why you need to know how much risk you can stomach before you start looking for investments and buying them online.

TIP: Several excellent online tools can help you get a handle on how much of a financial thrill seeker you are. Most are structured like interviews that ask you a number of questions and help you decide how much volatility you can comfortably stomach. These interviews are kind of like personality tests for your investment taste. Answering these questionnaires right away will help you understand what kind of investor you are:

- **Vanguard's Investor Questionnaire** (`https://personal.vanguard.com/us/FundsInvQuestionnaire`) asks ten salient questions to determine how much of a risk taker you are with your money. It determines your ideal *asset allocation* (a fancy term for an investing road map). Take note of the breakdown. The closer to 100 percent that Vanguard recommends you put in stocks, the more risk-tolerant you are, and the closer to 100 percent in bonds, the less risk-tolerant you are.

- **Index Funds Advisors Risk Capacity Survey** (`www.ifa.com/SurveyNET/index.aspx`) offers a quick risk survey that can tell you what kind of investor you are after answering just five questions. You can also find a complete risk capacity survey that hits you with a few dozen questions. Whichever you choose, the survey can characterize what kind of investor you are and even display a painting that portrays your risk tolerance.
- **Charles Schwab Investor Profile Questionnaire** (`www.schwab.com/resource/investment-questionnaire`) gets you to think about the factors that greatly determine how you should be investing, such as your investment time horizon and tolerance for risk. The Schwab questionnaire can be printed so you don't have to be in front of a computer to take it. At the bottom of the questionnaire is a chart that helps you see how aggressive or conservative you should be with your portfolio.

Approach investing like a chef with a recipe in hand. Instead of tossing all sorts of ingredients into your portfolio pot and guessing what it will taste like, it's best to know what needs to go into the pot to get what you want. In investing, this plan is called an *asset allocation.*

An asset allocation might be general and tell you what percentage of holdings to put in stocks, bonds, and cash. But it can also get more detailed and exotic, calling for a dash of large Canadian company stocks, a pinch of international stocks, and just a touch of emerging markets.

Asset allocations are designed to let all the investments in your portfolio blend together into a stew that will be most likely to generate the highest possible return for the lowest amount of risk.

The advantages of creating and sticking with an asset allocation include

- **Diversification:** Hands down, diversification is the biggest advantage of having an asset allocation. An asset allocation calls for certain percentages of your portfolio to be in certain investments. For instance, you might put 70 percent in stocks and 30 percent in bonds. You want your investments to be spread into different investments that tend to move up and down at different times. This diversification will hold the value of your total portfolio steady — and reduce risk — over time.

- **Rebalancing:** A great way to boost your returns without taking on additional risk, rebalancing pretty much does what the term implies. Periodically, one group of investments in your asset allocation will fall in value. Stocks might fall and bonds rally, for instance. When that happens, the percentage of your portfolio in stocks will fall below your plan and the percentage in bonds will rise. To stick to your allocation and maintain the percentages, you need to buy more of the investments that have fallen in value and sell those that have gained. And when you do that, you'll be buying investments when they're cheaper and selling them when they get pricier, which isn't a bad strategy.
- **Discipline:** Staying in control is priceless with online investing. Because trading online is so inexpensive and easy, it's tempting to chase after popular stocks that are in the news or new investments other investors are talking about. Many of those investments end up disappointing investors, though, because they're overvalued. If you stick with your asset allocation, you can avoid this pain.

What Kind of Investor Do You Plan to Be?

Investing might not seem controversial, but it shouldn't surprise you that anytime you're talking about money, people have some strong opinions about the right way to do things. The first way investors categorize themselves is by whether they are passive or active. Because these two approaches are so different, the following sections help you think about what they are and which camp you see yourself in.

How to know if you're a passive investor

Passive investors don't try to beat the stock market. They merely try to keep up with it by owning all the stocks in an index. An *index* is a basket of stocks or bonds that track a market by measuring movement by all the investments in it. For instance, the S&P/TSX Composite Index tracks about 250 of the biggest Canadian companies listed on the Canadian Stock Exchange (TSX). Passive investors are happy matching the market's performance.

TIP You know you're a passive investor if you

- **Aren't interested in choosing individual stocks:** These investors buy large baskets of stocks that mirror the performance of popular stock indexes. Passive investors don't worry if a small upstart company they invested in will release its new product on time and whether it will be well received. They typically own small pieces of hundreds of stocks instead.

- **Want to own mutual funds and exchange-traded funds:** Because passive investors aren't looking for the next Apple or Microsoft, they buy mutual and exchange-traded funds that buy hundreds of stocks.

  Mutual funds pool money from many investors so it can then be invested in stocks, bonds, or other assets. By pooling money, mutual funds give many investors some of the benefits that larger investors enjoy, especially the ability to spread money over multiple investments, or *diversify.*

  Like index mutual funds, most *exchange-traded funds* (ETFs; see Chapter 2) invest in baskets of stocks tied to a stock market index. ETFs have proven to be so popular that new types are constantly being created, including variants that own investments in commodities or stocks picked by money managers. ETFs differ from mutual funds in several key ways, including that they trade during the day just like an individual stock and have potential tax advantages over mutual funds. These important differences give ETFs an edge over mutual funds for some investors.

- **Want to reduce taxes:** Passive investors tend to buy investments and forget about them until many years later when they need the money. This approach can be lucrative because by holding onto diversified investments for a long time and not selling them, passive investors can postpone when they have to pay taxes.
- **Do not want to stress about stocks' daily, monthly, or even annual movements:** Passive investors tend to buy index or mutual funds and forget about them. They don't need to sit in front of financial TV shows, surf countless financial websites, read magazines, or worry about where stocks are moving. They're invested for the long term, and everything else is just noise to them.

Sites for passive investors to start with

One of the toughest things about being a passive investor is sitting still during a bull market when everyone else seems to be making more than you. Yes, you might be able to turn off the TV, but inevitably you'll bump into someone who brags about their giant gains and laughs at you for being satisfied with 10 percent average annual market returns.

TIP When that happens, it's even more important to stick with your philosophy. Following the crowd at this moment undermines the value of your strategy. That's why even passive investors are well served going to websites where other passive investors congregate:

- **Bogleheads** (www.bogleheads.org) is an electronic water cooler for fans of Vanguard index funds and passive investors to meet, encourage, and advise each other. They call themselves Bogleheads in honor of the founder of Vanguard, John Bogle.
- **The Arithmetic of Active Management** (www.stanford.edu/~wfsharpe/art/active/active.htm) is a reprint of an article by an early proponent of passive investing, William Sharpe, who explains why active investing can never win.
- **Vanguard** (www.vanguard.ca/en/investor/home) contains many helpful stories about the power of index investing and offers them for free, even if you don't have an account.

How to know whether you're an active investor

Active investors almost feel sorry for passive investors. Why would anyone be satisfied just matching the stock market and not even try to do better? Active investors feel that if you're smart enough and willing to spend time doing homework, you can exceed 10 percent annual returns. Likewise, active investors question the logic of holding stocks even as markets plunge. Active investors also find investing to be thrilling, almost like a hobby. Some active investors try to find undervalued stocks and hold them until they're discovered by other investors. Another class of active investors are short-term traders, who bounce in and out of stocks trying to get quick gains.

You're an active investor if you

- **Think long-term averages of stocks are meaningless:** Active investors believe they can spot winning companies that no one knows about yet or are underappreciated, buy their shares at just the right time, and sell them for a profit.
- **Are willing to spend a lot of time searching for stocks:** These are the investors who sit in front of financial TV shows, analyze stocks that look undervalued, and do all sorts of prospecting trying to find gems.
- **Believe they can hire mutual fund managers who can beat the market:** Some active investors think that certain talented mutual fund managers are out there and that if they just give their money to those managers, they'll win.
- **Suspect certain types of stocks aren't priced correctly and many investors make bad decisions:** Active investors believe they can outsmart the masses and routinely capitalize on their mistakes of the great unwashed.

- **Understand the risks:** Most active traders underperform index funds, some without even realizing it. Before deciding to be an active trader, be sure to test out your skills with online simulations, or make sure that you're measuring your performance correctly. If you're losing money picking stocks, stop doing it.

TIP

Here's a quick method for measuring your performance correctly. If you haven't deposited money into or taken any money out of your brokerage account, it's relatively easy to measure your rate of return for the year. Just follow these steps:

1. **Get your account balance at the end of the year and write it down.**

   You can get your year-end balance from your online broker's website or from a printed statement.

2. **Get your account balance at the end of the previous year and write it down.**

   Again, this information is available from your broker's website or from a printed statement.

3. **Subtract the answer in Step 2 from the answer in Step 1.**

4. **Divide the answer in Step 3 by the answer in Step 2, and then multiply by 100.**

Say your portfolio was worth $12,000 on December 31, 2021, and $10,000 on December 31, 2020. You would subtract $10,000 from $12,000 and get $2,000. Divide $2,000 by $10,000 and multiply by 100, and the answer is 20 percent. You earned a 20 percent rate of return in that year.

TIP: Don't worry about dividends and splits when using this approach. And don't concern yourself if you've bought or sold stocks. As long as your dividends and sale proceeds go into the brokerage account, this way of calculating your return reflects all these things.

Many investors try, but few are able to consistently beat the market. Consider Bill Miller, portfolio manager for the Legg Mason Capital Management Value Trust mutual fund. Miller had beaten the market for 15 years and turned into a poster child for active investors, proof that beating the market was possible if you were smart enough. But even Miller's streak came to an end in 2006. That's when his Legg Mason Value Trust fund didn't just trail the market, it lagged by a mile, returning just 5.9 percent while the market gained 15.8 percent. The fund lagged the market in 2007 by 12.2 percent and again in 2008 by 18.1 percent. While the fund beat the market in 2009, active investors had already lost their hero. Even now, more than a decade later, there's yet to be a mutual fund with an equivalent record.

Sites for the active investor to start with

Ever hear of someone trying to learn a foreign language by moving to the country and picking it up through immersion? The idea is that by just being around the language, and through the necessity of buying food or finding the restroom, the person eventually gets proficient.

If you're interested in active investing, you can do the same thing by hitting websites that are common hangouts for active investors and picking up how these types of investors find stocks that interest them and trade on them. These sites can show you the great pains active investors go through in their attempt to beat the market. Here are a few to start looking at:

- **TheStreet.com** (`www.thestreet.com`) collects trading ideas and tips from writers mainly looking for quick-moving stocks and other investments.
- **Investor's Business Daily** (`www.investors.com`) provides tools and research for investors looking for promising stocks. The site highlights stocks that have moved up or down by a large amount, which usually catches the attention of traders.
- **Seeking Alpha** (`http://seekingalpha.com`) provides news and commentary for investors of all skill levels who are trying to beat the market.

2

The Basics of ETFs

Banking your retirement on stocks is risky enough; banking your retirement on any individual stock, or even a handful of stocks, is about as risky as wrestling crocodiles. Banking on individual bonds is less risky, but the same general principle holds: There is safety in numbers. That's why teenage boys and girls huddle together in corners at school dances. That's why gnus graze in groups. That's why smart stock and bond investors grab onto exchange-traded funds (ETFs).

In this chapter, we explain not only the safety features of ETFs but also the ways in which they differ from their cousins, mutual funds. After reading this chapter, you should have a pretty good idea of what ETFs can do for your portfolio.

ETFs versus Mutual Funds and Stocks

So, what is the difference between an ETF and a mutual fund? After all, mutual funds also represent baskets of stocks or bonds. The two, however, are not twins. They're not even siblings. Cousins are more like it. Here are some of the big differences between ETFs and mutual funds:

- ETFs are bought and sold just like stocks (through a brokerage house, either by phone or online), and their prices change throughout the trading day. Mutual fund orders can be made during the day, but the actual trading doesn't occur until after the markets close.
- ETFs tend to represent *indexes* (market segments) and the managers of the ETFs tend to do very little trading of securities in the ETF. (The ETFs are passively managed.) Most mutual funds are actively managed.
- Although they may require you to pay small trading fees, ETFs usually wind up costing you much less than mutual funds because the ongoing management fees are typically much lower, and there is never a *load*

(an entrance and/or exit fee, sometimes an exorbitant one), as you find with many mutual funds.

- Because of low portfolio turnover and also the way ETFs are structured, ETFs generally declare much less in taxable capital gains than mutual funds do.

Table 2-1 provides a quick look at some ways that investing in ETFs differs from investing in mutual funds and individual stocks.

	ETFs	Mutual Funds	Individual Stocks
Are they priced, bought, and sold throughout the day?	Yes	No	Yes
Do they offer some investment diversification?	Yes	Yes	No
Is there a minimum investment?	Yes	Yes	Yes
Are they purchased through a broker or online brokerage?	Yes	Yes	Yes
Do you pay a fee or commission to make a trade?	Rarely	Sometimes	Rarely
Can that fee or commission be more than a few dollars?	No	Yes	No
Can you buy or sell options?	Sometimes	No	Sometimes
Are they indexed (passively managed)?	Typically	Atypically	No
Can you make money or lose money?	Yes	Yes	You bet

Table 2-1: *ETFs versus Mutual Funds versus Individual Stocks*

Why Individual Investors Are Learning to Love ETFs

Low costs are probably what we love most about ETFs. But we also love their tax efficiency, transparency (you know what you're buying), and good track record of success.

The cost advantage: How low can you go?

In the world of actively managed mutual funds (which is to say, most mutual funds), the average annual management fee, according to the Investment Company Institute and Morningstar, is 0.63 percent of the account balance. That may not sound like a lot, but don't be misled. A well-balanced portfolio with both stocks and bonds may return, say, 5 percent over time. In that case, paying 0.63 percent to a third party means that you've just lowered your total investment returns by one-eighth. In a bad year, when your investments earn, say, 0.63 percent, you've just lowered your investment returns to *zero*. And in a *very* bad year, you don't need us to do the math.

Active ETFs, although cheaper than active mutual funds, aren't all that much cheaper, averaging 0.51 percent a year, although a few are considerably higher than that.

We're astounded at what some funds charge. Whereas the average active fund charges between 0.51 percent (for ETFs) and 0.63 percent (for mutual funds), we've seen charges five times that amount! Crazy. Investing in such a fund is tossing money to the wind. Yet people do it. The chances of your winding up ahead after paying such high fees are next to nil. Paying a load that can total as much as 6 percent is just as nutty. Yet people do it.

In the world of index funds, the expenses are much lower, with index mutual funds averaging 0.06 percent and ETFs averaging 0.17 percent, although many of the more traditional indexed ETFs cost no more than 0.06 percent a year in management fees, and as more competition has entered the market, even that price now seems high. A handful are now under 0.03 percent. And one purveyor, BNY Mellon, has actually introduced two ETFs with *no* fees.

The management companies that bring us ETFs, such as BlackRock and Invesco, are presumably not doing so for their health. No, they're making a good profit. One reason they can offer ETFs so cheaply compared to mutual funds is that their expenses are much lower. When you buy an ETF, you go through a brokerage house, not BlackRock or Invesco. That brokerage house does all the necessary paperwork and bookkeeping on the purchase. If you have any questions about your money, you'll likely call the brokerage house, not BlackRock. So, unlike a mutual fund company, which must maintain phone operators, bookkeepers, and a mailroom, the providers of ETFs can operate almost entirely in cyberspace.

ETFs that are linked to indexes do have to pay some kind of fee to whoever created the index. But that fee is *nothing* compared to the exorbitant salaries that mutual funds pay their dart throwers, er, stock pickers, er, market analysts.

Tax talk

Alas, unless your money is in a tax-advantaged retirement account, making money in the markets means that you have to fork over something to the government at the end of the year. That's true, of course, whether you invest in individual securities or funds. But before there were ETFs, individual securities had a big advantage over funds in that you were required to pay capital gains taxes only when you actually enjoyed a capital gain. With mutual funds, that isn't so. The fund itself may realize a capital gain by selling off an appreciated stock. You pay the capital gains tax regardless of whether you sell anything and regardless of whether the share price of the mutual fund increased or decreased since the time you bought it.

There have been times (pick a bad year for the market — 2000, 2008, and so on) when many mutual fund investors lost a considerable amount in the market yet had to pay capital gains taxes at the end of the year. Talk about adding insult to injury! One study found that over the course of time, taxes have wiped out approximately 2 full percentage points in returns for investors in the highest tax brackets.

In the world of ETFs, such losses are very unlikely to happen. Because most ETFs are index-based, they generally have little turnover to create capital gains. Perhaps even more important, ETFs are structured in a way that largely insulates shareholders from capital gains that result when mutual funds are forced to sell in order to free up cash to pay off shareholders who cash in their chips.

TIP

The structure of ETFs makes them different than mutual funds. Actually, ETFs are legally structured in three different ways: as exchange-traded, open-end mutual funds; as exchange-traded unit investment trusts; and as exchange-traded grantor trusts. The differences are subtle. For now, we want to focus on one seminal difference between ETFs and mutual funds, which boils down to an extremely clever setup whereby ETF shares, which represent stock holdings, can be traded without any actual trading of stocks.

Think of the poker player who plays hand after hand, but thanks to the miracle of little plastic chips, doesn't have to touch any cash.

In the world of ETFs, you don't have croupiers, but you have *market makers*, people who work at the stock exchanges and create (like magic!) ETF shares. Each ETF share represents a portion of a portfolio of stocks, sort of like poker chips represent a pile of cash. As an ETF grows, so does the number of shares. Concurrently (once a day), new stocks are added to a portfolio that mirrors the ETF.

When an ETF investor sells shares, those shares are bought by a market maker who turns around and sells them to another ETF investor. By contrast, with mutual funds, if one person sells, the mutual fund must sell off shares of the underlying stock to pay off the shareholder. If stocks sold in the mutual fund are being sold for more than the original purchase price, the shareholders left behind are stuck paying a capital gains tax. In some years, that amount can be substantial.

In the world of ETFs, no such thing has happened or is likely to happen, at least not with the vast majority of ETFs, which are index funds. Because index funds trade infrequently, and because of ETFs' poker-chip structure, ETF investors rarely see a bill from the government for any capital gains tax. That's not a guarantee that there will never be capital gains on any index ETF, but if there ever are, they're sure to be minor.

The actively managed ETFs — currently a small fraction of the ETF market, but almost certain to grow — may present a somewhat different story. They're going to be, no doubt, less tax friendly than index ETFs but more tax friendly than actively managed mutual funds. Exactly where will they fall on the spectrum? It may take another few years before we really know.

Tax efficient does not mean tax-free. Although you won't pay capital gains taxes, you will pay taxes on any dividends issued by your stock ETFs, and stock ETFs are just as likely to issue dividends as mutual funds are. In addition, if you sell your ETFs and they're in a taxable account, you have to pay capital gains tax if the ETFs have appreciated in value since the time you bought them. But hey, at least you get to decide when to take a gain, and when you do, it's an actual gain.

ETFs that invest in taxable bonds and throw off taxable-bond interest are not likely to be very much more tax friendly than taxable-bond mutual funds.

ETFs that invest in actual commodities, holding real silver or gold, tax you at the "collectible" rate. And ETFs that tap into derivatives (such as commodity futures) and currencies sometimes bring with them very complex (and costly) tax issues.

TIP

Taxes on earnings — be they dividends or interest or money made on currency swaps — aren't an issue if your money is held in a tax-advantaged account. Also, keep in mind the significant tax difference in short-term and long-term capital gains. Long-term capital gains (holding your asset or security for at least a full year and a day) means paying a more favorable tax rate. See your tax advisor for more details.

What you see is what you get

A key to building a successful portfolio, right up there with low costs and tax efficiency, is diversification. You can't diversify optimally unless you know exactly what's in your portfolio. In a rather infamous example, when tech stocks (some more than others) started to go belly up in 2000, holders of Janus mutual funds got clobbered. That's because they learned after the fact that their three or four Janus mutual funds, which gave the illusion of diversification, were actually holding many of the same stocks.

With a mutual fund, you often have little idea of what stocks the fund manager is holding. In fact, you may not even know what *kinds* of stocks they're holding — or even if they are holding stocks! We're talking here about *style drift,* which occurs when a mutual fund manager advertises their fund as aggressive, but over time it becomes conservative, and vice versa. We're talking about mutual fund managers who say they love large value but invest in large growth or small value.

When you buy an indexed ETF, you get complete transparency. You know exactly what you're buying. No matter what the ETF, you can see in the prospectus or on the ETF provider's website (or on any number of independent financial websites) a complete picture of the ETF's holdings. See, for example, `http://finance.yahoo.com`. If you go to that website and type the letters *XIC* (the ticker symbol for the iShares Core S&P/TSX Capped Composite Index ETF) in the box in the upper-right corner of the screen, you can see in an instant what your holdings are. You simply can't get that information on most actively managed mutual funds. Or, if you can, the information is both stale and subject to change without notice.

The scandals that have rocked the mutual fund world over the years have left the world of ETFs untouched. There's not a whole lot of manipulation that a fund manager can do when their picks are tied to an index. And because ETFs trade throughout the day, with the price flashing across thousands of computer screens worldwide, there is no room to take advantage of the "stale" pricing that occurs after the markets close and mutual fund orders are settled. All in all, ETF investors are much less likely ever to get bamboozled than are investors in active mutual funds.

Do ETFs Belong in Your Life?

Okay, so on the plus side of ETFs, you have ultra-low management expenses, super tax efficiency, transparency, and a lot of fancy trading opportunities, such as shorting, if you're so inclined. What about the negatives? The following sections walk you through some other facts about ETFs that you should consider before parting with your precious dollars.

Calculate commissions

You may have to pay a commission every time you buy and sell an ETF. But, as we're writing these words, another brokerage house may have eliminated commissions altogether.

Trading commissions for stocks and ETFs (it's the same commission for either) have been dropping faster than the price of desktop computers. What once would have cost you a bundle, now — if you trade online, which you definitely should — is really pin money, perhaps a few dollars a trade, and increasingly, nothing at all. So, unless you're investing a very small amount of money, you don't need to worry about commissions anymore.

Move money in a flash

The fact that ETFs can be traded throughout the day like stocks makes them, unlike mutual funds, fair game for day traders and institutional wheeler-dealers. For the rest of us common folk, there isn't much about the way that ETFs are bought and sold that makes them especially valuable. Indeed, the ability to trade throughout the day may make you more apt to do so, perhaps selling or buying on impulse. Impulsive investing, although it can get your endorphins pumping, is generally not a profitable way to proceed.

Understand tracking error

At times, the return of an ETF may be greater or less than the index it follows. This situation is called *tracking error.* At times, an ETF may also sell at a price that is a tad higher or lower than what that price should be, given the prices of all the securities held by the ETF. This situation is called selling at a *premium* (when the price of the ETF rides above the value of the securities) or selling at a *discount* (when the price of the ETF drops below the value of the securities). Both foreign-stock funds and bond funds are more likely to run off track, either experiencing tracking errors or selling at a premium or discount. But the better funds don't run off track to any alarming degree.

TIP: Minimizing "off-track" ETF investing is not something to worry about if you're a buy-and-hold ETF investor — the kind of investor you should become.

Make a sometimes tricky choice

Here are a couple of very basic examples of decisions you may be facing as you construct a portfolio that meets your needs.

Say you have a choice between investing in an index mutual fund that charges 0.06 percent a year and an ETF that tracks the same index and charges the same amount. Or, say you're trying to choose between an actively managed mutual fund and an ETF with the very same manager managing the very same kind of investment, with the same costs. What should you invest in?

TIP: If your money is in a taxable account, and you're looking at stock index funds, go with the ETF, provided there are no commissions to pay; it may wind up being more tax efficient. If you're looking at bond index funds, this decision is a flip of the coin. Managed funds? Same.

But what if your brokerage still charges a commission? Avoid it by going with the mutual fund (provided the mutual fund doesn't cost you a commission). What if there's a difference in management fees between the two funds? Say, an ETF charges you a management fee of 0.1 percent a year, and a comparable index mutual fund charges 0.15 percent, but buying and selling the ETF will cost you $5 at either end. For this example, say you have $5,000 to invest. Now what should you do?

The math isn't difficult. The difference between 0.1 and 0.15 (0.05 percent) of $5,000 is $2.50. It will take you two years to recoup your trading fee of $5. If you factor in the cost of selling (another $5), it will take you four years to recoup your trading costs. At that point, the ETF will be your lower-cost tortoise, and the mutual fund will be your higher-cost hare.

TIP

If you have a trigger finger, and you're the kind of person who is likely to jump to trade every time there's a blip in the market, you would be well advised to go with mutual funds (that don't impose short-term redemption fees). You're less likely to shoot yourself in the foot!

3

What Is a Cryptocurrency?

So you've turned to this chapter, and your first question is probably this: "What the heck is a cryptocurrency, anyway?" Simply stated, a *cryptocurrency* is a new form of digital money. You can transfer your traditional, non-cryptocurrency money (like the Canadian dollar) digitally, but that's not quite the same as how cryptocurrencies work. When cryptocurrencies become mainstream, you may be able to use them to pay for stuff electronically, just as you do with traditional currencies.

However, what sets cryptocurrencies apart is the technology behind them. You may say, "Who cares about the technology behind my money? I only care about how much of it there is in my wallet!" The issue is that the world's current money systems have a bunch of problems. Here are some examples:

- Payment systems such as credit cards and wire transfers are outdated.
- In most cases, a bunch of middlemen, like banks and brokers, take a cut in the process, making transactions expensive and slow.
- Financial inequality is growing around the globe.
- Billions of unbanked or underbanked people can't access financial services. That's approximately half the population on the planet!

Cryptocurrencies aim to solve some of these problems, if not more. This chapter introduces you to crypto fundamentals.

The Basics of Cryptocurrencies

You know how your everyday, government-based currency is reserved in banks? And that you need an ATM or a connection to a bank to get more of it or transfer it to other people?

Well, with cryptocurrencies, you may be able to get rid of banks and other centralized middlemen altogether. That's because cryptocurrencies rely on a technology called *blockchain*, which is *decentralized* (meaning no single entity is in charge of it). Instead, every computer in the network confirms the transactions.

Simply put, a *blockchain* is a special kind of database. According to `www.cigionline.org/multimedia/what-blockchain`, the term *blockchain* refers to the whole network of distributed ledger technologies. According to Oxford Dictionaries, a *ledger* is "a book or other collection of financial accounts of a particular type." It can be a computer file that records transactions. A ledger is actually the foundation of accounting and is as old as writing and money.

Now imagine a whole suite of incorruptible digital ledgers of economic transactions that can be programmed to record and track not only financial transactions but also virtually everything of value. The blockchain can track things like medical records, land titles, and even voting. It's a shared, distributed, and immutable ledger that records the history of transactions starting with transaction number one. It establishes trust, accountability, and transparency.

TIP

Blockchain stores information in batches called *blocks.* These blocks are linked together in a sequential way to form a continuous line. A chain of blocks. A blockchain. Each block is like a page of a ledger or a record book. Each block mainly has three elements:

- **Data:** The type of data depends on what the blockchain is being used for. In Bitcoin, for example, a block's data contains the details about the transaction, including sender, receiver, number of coins, and so on.

- **Hash:** A *hash* in blockchain is something like a fingerprint or signature. It identifies a block and all its content, and it's always unique.
- **Hash of previous block:** This piece is precisely what makes a blockchain! Because each block carries the information of the previous block, the chain becomes very secure.

In the following sections, we go over more of the basics of cryptocurrencies: their background, benefits, and more.

The definition of money

Before getting into the nitty-gritty of cryptocurrencies, you need to understand the definition of money itself. The philosophy behind money is a bit like the whole "Which came first: the chicken or the egg?" thing. In order for money to be valuable, it must have a number of characteristics, such as the following:

- Enough people must have it.
- Merchants must accept it as a form of payment.
- Society must trust that it's valuable and that it will remain valuable in the future.

Of course, in the old days, when you traded your chicken for shoes, the values of the exchanged materials were inherent to their nature. But when coins, cash, and credit cards came into play, the definition of money and, more important, the trust model of money changed.

Another key change in money has been its ease of transaction. The hassle of carrying a ton of gold bars from one country to another was one of the main reasons cash was invented. Then, when people got even lazier, credit cards were invented. But credit cards carry the money that your government controls.

As the world becomes more interconnected and more concerned about authorities who may or may not have people's best interests in mind, cryptocurrencies may offer a valuable alternative.

Here's a fun fact: Your normal, government-backed currency, such as the Canadian dollar, must go by its fancy name, *fiat currency,* now that cryptocurrencies are around. Fiat is described as a legal tender like coins and banknotes that have value only because the government says so.

Some cryptocurrency history

The first ever cryptocurrency was Bitcoin. You've probably heard of Bitcoin more than any other thing in the crypto industry. Bitcoin was the first product of the first blockchain developed by some anonymous entity who went by the name Satoshi Nakamoto. Satoshi released the idea of Bitcoin in 2008 and described it as a "purely peer-to-peer version" of electronic money. (See Chapter 4 for more about Bitcoin.)

Bitcoin was the first established cryptocurrency, but many attempts at creating digital currencies occurred years before Bitcoin was formally introduced.

Cryptocurrencies like Bitcoin are created through a process called *mining*. Very different than mining ore, mining cryptocurrencies involves powerful computers solving complicated problems. Bitcoin and other minable cryptocurrencies rely on miners to maintain their network. By solving math problems and providing consent on the validity of transactions, miners support the blockchain network, which will otherwise collapse. For their service to the network, miners are rewarded with newly created cryptocurrencies (such as Bitcoins) and transaction fees.

Bitcoin remained the only cryptocurrency until 2011. Then Bitcoin enthusiasts started noticing flaws in it, so they decided to create alternative coins, also known as *altcoins*, to improve Bitcoin's design for things like speed, security, anonymity, and more. Among the first altcoins was Litecoin, which aimed to become the silver to Bitcoin's gold. But as of the time of writing, thousands of cryptocurrencies are available, and the number is expected to increase in the future.

Key crypto benefits

Still not convinced that cryptocurrencies (or any other sort of decentralized money) are a better solution than traditional government-based money? Here are a number of solutions that cryptocurrencies may be able to provide through their decentralized nature:

- **Reducing corruption:** With great power comes great responsibility. But when you give a ton of power to only one person or entity, the chances of their abusing that power increase. The 19th-century British politician Lord Acton said it best: "Power tends to corrupt, and absolute power corrupts absolutely." Cryptocurrencies aim to resolve the issue of absolute power by distributing power among many people or, better yet, among all the members of the network. That's the key idea behind blockchain technology anyway.
- **Eliminating extreme money printing:** Governments have central banks, and central banks have the ability to simply print money when they're faced with a serious economic problem. This process is also called *quantitative easing*. By printing more money, a government may be able to bail out debt or devalue its currency. However, this approach is like putting a bandage on a broken leg. Not only does it rarely solve the problem,

but the negative side effects also can sometimes surpass the original issue.

For example, when a country like Iran or Venezuela prints too much money, the value of its currency drops so much that inflation skyrockets and people can't even afford to buy everyday goods and services. Their cash becomes barely as valuable as rolls of toilet paper. Most cryptocurrencies have a limited, set amount of coins available. When all those coins are in circulation, a central entity or the company behind the blockchain has no easy way to simply create more coins or add on to its supply.

- **Giving people charge of their own money:** With traditional cash, you're basically giving away all your control to central banks and the government. If you trust your government, that's great, but keep in mind that at any point, your government is able to simply freeze your bank account and deny your access to your funds. For example, in the United States, if you don't have a legal will and own a business, the government has the right to all your assets if you pass away. Some governments can even simply abolish bank notes the way India did in 2016. With cryptocurrencies, you and only you can access your funds. (Unless someone steals them from you, that is.)

- **Cutting out the middleman:** With traditional money, every time you make a transfer, a middleman like your bank or a digital payment service takes a cut. With cryptocurrencies, all the network members in the blockchain are that middleman; their compensation is formulated differently from that of fiat money middlemen's and, therefore, is minimal in comparison.
- **Serving the unbanked:** A vast portion of the world's citizens has no access or limited access to payment systems like banks. Cryptocurrencies aim to resolve this issue by spreading digital commerce around the globe so that anyone with a mobile phone can start making payments. And yes, more people have access to mobile phones than to banks. In fact, more people have mobile phones than have toilets, but at this point the blockchain technology may not be able to resolve the latter issue.

Common crypto and blockchain myths

TIP During the 2017 Bitcoin hype, a lot of misconceptions about the whole industry started to circulate. These myths may have played a role in the cryptocurrency crash that followed the surge. The important thing to remember is that both the blockchain technology and its by-product, the cryptocurrency market, are still in their infancy, and things are rapidly changing. Let's get some of the most common misunderstandings out of the way:

- **Cryptocurrencies are good only for criminals.** Some cryptocurrencies boast anonymity as one of their key features. That means your identity isn't revealed when you're making transactions. Other cryptocurrencies are based on a decentralized blockchain, meaning a central government isn't the sole power behind them. These features do make such cryptocurrencies attractive for criminals; however, law-abiding citizens in corrupt countries can also benefit from them. For example, if you don't trust your local bank or country because of corruption and political instability, the best way to store your money may be through the blockchain and cryptocurrency assets.
- **You can make anonymous transactions using all cryptocurrencies.** For some reason, many people equate Bitcoin with anonymity. But Bitcoin, along with many other cryptocurrencies, doesn't incorporate anonymity at all. All transactions made using such cryptocurrencies are made on public blockchain. Some cryptocurrencies, such as Monero, do prioritize privacy, meaning no outsider can find the source, amount, or destination

of transactions. However, most other cryptocurrencies, including Bitcoin, don't operate that way.

- **The only application of blockchain is Bitcoin.** This idea couldn't be further from the truth. Bitcoin and other cryptocurrencies are a tiny by-product of the blockchain revolution. Many people believe Satoshi created Bitcoin simply to provide an example of how the blockchain technology can work. Almost every industry and business in the world can use the blockchain technology in its specific field.
- **All blockchain activity is private.** Many people falsely believe that the blockchain technology isn't open to the public and is accessible only to its network of common users. Although some companies create their own private blockchains to be used only among employees and business partners, the majority of the blockchains behind famous cryptocurrencies such as Bitcoin are accessible by the public. Literally anyone with a computer can access the transactions in real time. For example, you can view the real-time Bitcoin transactions at `www.blockchain.com`.

Risks

Just like anything else in life, cryptocurrencies come with their own baggage of risk. Whether you trade cryptos, invest in them, or simply hold onto them for the future, you must assess and understand the risks beforehand. Some of the most talked-about cryptocurrency risks include their volatility and lack of regulation. Volatility got especially out of hand in 2017, when the price of most major cryptocurrencies, including Bitcoin, skyrocketed above 1,000 percent and then came crashing down. However, as the cryptocurrency hype has calmed down, the price fluctuations have become more predictable and followed similar patterns of stocks and other financial assets.

Regulations are another major topic in the industry. The funny thing is that both lack of regulation and exposure to regulations can turn into risk events for cryptocurrency investors.

How to Choose an Exchange

The Internet has no lack of cryptocurrency exchanges. And more variations of exchanges are bound to make their way into the market. Which type of exchange is best for you: centralized exchange (CEX), decentralized exchange (DEX), or hybrid? Even then, which one of the many exchanges in each category should you choose?

We can't give you a solid answer for these questions, but we can offer ways to cycle through some of the most important characteristics in an exchange to help you make the best decision. The following sections note a few things to consider when choosing a cryptocurrency exchange.

First-time traders are better off doing their research on the cryptocurrencies first and then choosing an exchange. But once you become more experienced, you can simply choose cryptos to trade based on the current market conditions.

Because many of these exchanges offer different sets of pros and cons, you may be wise to diversify your cryptocurrency activities across a number of exchanges, just as many people do when they go grocery shopping. You may go to one store for its better-quality meat but get all your pasta from another.

Security

Security is one of the biggest issues in the cryptocurrency industry. Exchanges are at constant risk of hacks, frauds, and pump-and-dump schemes. A *pump-and-dump scheme* is when someone encourages investors to buy a crypto asset in order to artificially inflate its value (the "pumping" part) and then sells their own assets at a high price (the "dumping" part). That is why one of the most important things to do before choosing your crypto shop(s) is to do your research. Word of mouth and online reviews on sites like Reddit or news organizations like *Forbes* are some of the ways to help you choose a legitimate and secure platform.

TIP Some of other safety features you must check on the exchange include the following:

- **Two-factor authentication (2FA):** *Two-factor authentication* is a method of confirming your claimed identity by using a combination of two different factors: something the exchange knows (like your password) and something it has (like a six-digit number it sends to your mobile phone or your email address for the second step of the verification).
- **Cold storage for the majority of funds:** The exchange stores your funds offline so risk of online hacking is lower.
- **Proof of reserve:** The exchange must be audited to verify that the total amount of funds held by the exchange matches the amount required to cover an anonymized set of customer balances.

Supported currencies (crypto and otherwise)

When you decide which of the thousands of available cryptocurrencies are right for you, you must make sure your exchange carries them.

Additionally, if you're looking to purchase cryptocurrencies for the first time, you probably need an exchange that allows you to deposit your country's fiat currency.

Some exchanges use solely cryptocurrency for purchases, and some allow you to use fiat currencies such as the Canadian dollar, the euro, or another currency.

Liquidity

Without sufficient liquidity, the prices and the speeds of your transactions may be compromised. After you decide which cryptocurrencies you want to purchase, make sure your exchange offers sufficient liquidity and trading volume for fast and easy transactions. Liquidity also ensures you're able to buy and sell without the cryptocurrency's price being significantly affected by big market movers. The more buyers and sellers there are, the more liquidity that exists.

TIP

The best way to measure an exchange's liquidity is to look up its most recent trading volume. CoinMarketCap (`https://coinmarketcap.com`) is one of the many cryptocurrency information websites that rank exchanges based on their volume and liquidity.

Fees

Exchanges charge their customers in a number of different ways. It would be great if they didn't, but exchanges aren't charities. Charging customers fees is precisely how they make money to stay in business. The most common method is taking a small percentage of the amount you trade. Most exchanges charge a percentage lower than 1 percent; to stay competitive, some exchanges go as low as around 0.2 percent. Often, a sliding scale decreases the fee percentage as the user's monthly trading volume rises.

Paying less is always attractive, but prioritize security and liquidity over the fees. Your investment will defeat its purpose if you pay next to nothing on transaction fees and then lose all your funds in a hacker's attack.

Ease of use

This one is especially important for newbies. You want your exchange to provide you with an easy-to-use, intuitive, and fast user interface. This factor also depends on what kind of device you want to use for your cryptocurrency investing activities. If you're always on the go, you may want to choose an exchange with great mobile app services.

A good user experience helps you take more informed and more efficient actions on the exchange. Another benefit of exchanges with great interface and mobile support is that they're more likely to grow more quickly and, therefore, provide more trading volume and liquidity in their markets.

Location

You may find a specific exchange that works better for you in Canada than another, more popular one on an international level does. Some of the things to keep in mind are issues like which fiat currency exchanges accept and what fees they charge locals compared to international customers.

Additionally, the location of the exchange dictates the laws it has to comply with. At the time of writing, many countries don't have any specific regulations on cryptocurrencies. However, if and when they start to regulate, any restrictions may significantly affect your ability to participate in the market through the exchanges in those countries.

Method of payment

Look into the methods of payment the exchange accepts. Some exchanges require deposits by bank transfer, some use PayPal, and some accept credit and debit cards. Typically, the easier it is for you to pay, the more fees you're going to have to pay. For example, few services allow you to pay with a credit or debit card, and the ones that do will make you pay for the convenience. (Head to the earlier section "Fees" for more on fee issues.) One example of such services is xCoins (`https://xcoins.io`), which accepts credit cards and PayPal to exchange Bitcoins. They call it "lending," but their concept is similar to buying and selling.

Customer support

You should feel comfortable knowing the place you're trusting with your funds has a responsive customer support service. You can check this factor either by directly contacting the customer support department and asking any questions that you haven't been able to find on the exchange's FAQ page or by perusing online cryptocurrency forums like the Bitcoin Forum (`https://bitcointalk.org`). You may find complaints about the exchanges in these forums. However, keep in mind that fast-growing exchanges often combat these complaints by improving their customer service, which is always a good thing.

TIP: Another point you may be able to find on forums is whether an exchange has spurred complaints about locking people out of their accounts. If it has, you may want to consider other options.

Trading options

Trading options are especially important for active and advanced traders. For example, depending on your risk tolerance and financial goals, you may want to have access to certain order types or margin trading. On these occasions, make sure you understand the risks involved with such trading activities before getting yourself in trouble.

Transaction limits

Most exchanges have a daily withdrawal/deposit limit. Unless you're an institutional trader who wants to make millions of transactions per day, these restrictions may not be an issue. But these limits are still something you may need to keep in mind, depending on your investing style and goals. You can typically find out about the exchanges' transaction limits on their websites without having to create an account.

How to Choose a Crypto Wallet

Depending on your cryptocurrency needs and goals, you may need more than one type of cryptocurrency wallet. For example, you may want to use cold wallets to store larger crypto reserves and hot wallets for active trading. Regardless, you can choose your cryptocurrency wallet(s) based on different characteristics, some of which we discuss in the following sections.

TIP: Make sure you've gathered everything you need to know about a given wallet before committing to getting one.

Based on security

Even if you're an active crypto trader, you should have a super-secure cold wallet where you store your larger amounts of crypto assets. Online wallets aren't the most secure option, however convenient they may be. You can always transfer your assets to an online wallet if you need immediate access to your cryptocurrencies for an investment/shopping opportunity.

Another point to keep in mind is that the most secure hardware wallets are normally the most expensive ones. So you should calculate whether spending that much money for a particular wallet makes sense for the amount of crypto you're going to store in it.

Some questions you must ask before choosing the most secure wallet include the following:

- What sort of authentication does the wallet use?
- Is the website secure?
- What do online reviews say?

TIP: CoinCentral (`https://coincentral.com`), 99Bitcoins (`https://99bitcoins.com`), and CryptoCompare (`https://www.cryptocompare.com`) are among the websites that provide an annual crypto wallet review. Check with two or more websites before making a decision.

TIP: At the time of writing, Ledger Nano S hardware wallet is one of the most popular and highly rated secure wallets out there. You can find out about other Ledger products at `www.ledger.com`. Trezor Bitcoin hardware wallet (created by SatoshiLabs) is another example. One catch about these is that if the USB drive dies, all your cryptos go with it. That's why you should always have a backup and keep your security codes elsewhere so you can recover your assets.

Based on your crypto ownership

Not all crypto wallets can handle your different types of cryptocurrency assets. In fact, some wallets are purpose-built for just one cryptocurrency; many cryptocurrencies have their own official wallets, which can handle only that one crypto. For example, Bitcoin-specific wallets include Bitcoin Core (`https://bitcoin.org/en/bitcoin-core`), Mycelium (`https://wallet.mycelium.com`), and Electrum (`https://electrum.org`). For Ethereum, you have options such as Guarda (`https://guarda.com`) and MyEtherWallet (which is a paper wallet; see `www.myetherwallet.com`). You can find more options at `www.ethereum.org/en/wallets`.

TIP

If you're not planning to diversify among other types of cryptocurrencies, a singular official cryptocurrency wallet may be right for you. Most of the time, you can find the official wallet of a cryptocurrency on the company's website.

Multicurrency wallets are an option for people who want to hold more than one cryptocurrency. The majority of online wallets provided on the exchanges give you the opportunity to store and transact among multiple cryptos. However, if you're using these wallets to store your crypto assets, know that your wallet security may be compromised.

TIP Do *not* leave your coins on an online exchange wallet.

Coinomi (`www.coinomi.com`) is a popular multicoin mobile wallet. It's a great multi-asset cryptocurrency wallet. Exodus (`www.exodus.com`) is another multicoin wallet. Your private keys remain secure on your device and never leave it. Exodus can even encrypt the private keys for you.

Based on transaction fees

If you're planning to do a lot of crypto shopping and use digital coins on the go, you may need to be mindful of the transaction fees you're paying along the way. This point is especially true for active traders. If you're a day trader and you're paying more on transaction fees than what you're making in the market, doesn't that defeat the purpose of trading?

Based on anonymity

Anonymity is an extra layer of security you can take into consideration when choosing a crypto wallet. If you use an anonymous wallet, you can separate your personal information from your funds, making it harder for anyone to track down your cryptos and potentially steal them. This factor is something that can be very personal. Some wallets offer full anonymity, while others don't. If anonymity is really important to you, choose among more-private wallets. Note that prioritizing anonymity may affect transaction fees and the price of the wallet.

TIP

To find the latest, most popular anonymous wallets, you can simply search the web for "anonymous cryptocurrency wallets." Anonymous wallets come in the forms of mobile, hardware, software, and so on. With that, you can have one or more anonymous wallets based on your needs. Some of the popular anonymous wallets at the time of writing include the following:

- **BitLox (`www.bitlox.com`):** This hardware Bitcoin wallet ensures both security and anonymity. It's capable of holding more than 100 wallets with the ability to create millions of addresses for each wallet.
- **Electrum (`https://electrum.org`):** This desktop Bitcoin wallet appears to be one of the software wallets most trusted by the cryptocurrency community.

- **Samourai (`https://samouraiwallet.com`):** This wallet is a mobile Bitcoin wallet. According to the Samourai website, the aim is to "to keep your transactions private, your identity masked, and your funds secure."

Fundamental Analysis for Picking Cryptocurrencies

Fundamental analysis is the art of using all the gossip, stories, and facts about a cryptocurrency, its financial situation, and upcoming risk events that may move the market. Finding the right crypto category is like picking your type in a significant other. Except in this case, you should most certainly think with your brain, and maybe a little bit with your gut feeling, but nothing more than that. Here are some methods you can use to cherry-pick the best cryptos for you.

Go with what you know

TIP

Going with what you know is a golden yet simple method also used in the stock market. If you've already been exposed to certain types of cryptocurrencies or, better yet, used them in real life and liked their performance, consider adding them to your portfolio.

In the stock market, for example, many newbie investors make several profitable investments by simply observing their own buying habits. If they prefer to buy from healthier fast-food services like Chipotle rather than McDonald's, they may consider adding Chipotle's stock to their portfolio.

Similarly, say you notice that your favorite online store has already added a cryptocurrency payment option to its checkout page and you place an order with it smoothly. That success may be an indication that the trading volume for that cryptocurrency will increase in the future, and the crypto may become a valuable asset for your portfolio.

Choose the right categories

Certain crypto categories perform better at certain times in the overall market, not just the crypto market. So, for example, if you notice that the financial technology (fintech) sector is heading higher in equities and that everyone is talking about artificial intelligence (AI), you may want to consider browsing through the AI category and finding cryptocurrencies that are involved with it.

Another way to pick the best categories for medium-term investments is to choose from categories that are already outperforming the overall market. We're not talking about a category that did well just today but rather something that either has been doing well for a few months or even years or is showing signs of picking up. You can pick the hottest category as your top pick and then add on the second and third ones for diversification purposes.

The cryptocurrency categories may not always follow the rest of the market. Because cryptocurrency is a new industry to begin with, you may find opportunities in it that you may not necessarily find in the more traditional equities market. Heck, the crypto industry may turn into the safety net if the stock market crashes.

TIP: *Exchange-traded funds* (ETFs; see Chapter 2) normally consist of a basket of a number of assets in the same category. They're super popular in the equities market because they make the choosing process much easier. They're also cheaper to purchase than their big, fancy hedge-fund equivalents, mutual funds. At the time of writing, cryptocurrency ETFs aren't really a thing yet. After cryptocurrency ETFs become popular, you can view and compare their charts to identify best-performing crypto categories.

Check out cryptos' websites

Whether you have a number of cryptocurrencies in mind based on your own experience or you've picked a category and you now want to choose the best crypto within that sector, you must now start a more detailed analysis on your finalists.

If you've ever watched *The Bachelor* or *The Bachelorette* on TV (guilty as charged), you're probably already familiar with the process. You start out with around 30 potential matches for your portfolio. By the time you're down to the three or four finalists, you're ready to see what their worlds are all about. In the cryptocurrency world, the company's website is the equivalent of the TV hometown dates. Here are a few ideas to consider when you're picking your crypto sweethearts that don't involve visiting their high schools and getting a grilling from their families.

Flip through their white papers

A *white paper* is something like a business proposal for new cryptocurrencies. It includes everything potential investors need to know about the crypto, such as technology, purpose, financial details, and so on. More-established cryptocurrencies may already have a page that breaks down all this critical information into easy-to-understand video clips and cool infographics on tabs titled "About" or "How It Works." For others, you may just need to find the white paper on the website and try to digest the information by reading. The good news is that white papers are often written in a language that people who aren't experts in the field can understand.

Identify their teams

No one really knows who created Bitcoin, but the rest of the cryptocurrencies out there normally have a team behind them that guides the company and its blockchain technology. The team behind the crypto is important even if its platform is completely open source, which means anyone can access and modify it.

When you invest in anything, whether it's stocks, a new start-up, or a hot date, understanding the background and how it came to life can play a major role. Here are some things to look for in the management:

- Bios
- Résumés
- Experience in the field

In addition to the core management, check the backgrounds of the members of the board of advisors if the company has it. You normally can find such information on the company's website, under tabs labeled things like "About Us" or "Our Team."

TIP

When you invest in a cryptocurrency, you're essentially investing in a start-up company and an entrepreneur. Sometimes these entrepreneurs are young with no qualifying résumé, just like Mark Zuckerberg (who founded Facebook, now known as Meta) was. That's when the creator's personality can become a factor in your decision making. As Mark Cuban (*Shark Tank* investor and Dallas Mavericks owner) told

CNBC, "When you invest in an entrepreneur, you get the personality. And if that's not appropriate or you don't think it's right, buy another stock" (or in this case, crypto).

Browse their partnerships

If you're not willing to take a lot of risk, seeing who in the industry has put their trust in the hands of the cryptocurrency you're considering buying is very important. More established cryptocurrencies have been able to team up with traditional giants like IBM and Microsoft and banks like Goldman Sachs. These companies have expert analytic teams perform due diligence before jumping on board with new investments and partnerships. Having reputable partners can be a sign that the company is solid and on the right track to get ahead of the competition.

Another good thing about having partners in the traditional world is that the cryptocurrency may have a higher chance of getting accepted by the masses. If a cryptocurrency has established partnerships with other companies, they're normally listed under a tab named "Our Partners" or "About Us."

Familiarize yourself with their technology

Many cryptocurrencies are tokens from blockchain companies with multiple products. Well-developed websites walk you through their technology and their products in a not-so-intimidating way. The more you get to know the products and the technology behind the cryptocurrency, the easier you can make your decision about the finalists on your cryptocurrency list.

Check out their contribution to society

What problems are your shortlist cryptocurrencies trying to solve? Does it matter to you? Are they just here to get rich quick, or do they have a long-term plan for the betterment of society? Finding an answer to these questions can also help you narrow down your list of finalists. Companies like Ripple describe their social contributions on a subtab called "Ripple for Good." Other companies often use a similar format or simply put their core social contributions first thing on their home page.

Analyze their road maps

TIP

Many companies behind cryptocurrencies have sections on their websites dedicated to their road maps: where they come from, what they've achieved, and what they're planning to accomplish in the future. If available, road maps are a great way to discover a ton of fundamental information about the crypto in a few minutes.

Get involved

Here's your lucky seven! Just like dating, the more you get involved, the more you get to know about the dirty secrets. The majority of cryptocurrency platforms love to increase their followings and encourage people to get involved right there on their websites. Depending on the cryptocurrency, getting involved can mean anything from mining to joining its social forums or even starting a new cryptocurrency project on its blockchain platform (like Ethereum)! Of course, getting involved also means investing more of your time, so you need to find a balance there.

Find additional resources

In addition to resources mentioned earlier in this chapter, check out the following for extensive guidance and education in addition to being able to transact in cryptocurrencies:

- Binance: `www.binance.com`
- Coinbase: `www.coinbase.com`
- CoinGecko: `www.coingecko.com`

Lastly, keep in mind that buying and selling cryptocurrencies has become as technically easy as buying stocks and ETFs in a brokerage account. Here are some popular brokers that make it easy:

- **eToro:** `www.etoro.com`
- **InvestinGoal:** `https://investingoal.com` (This site compares all the brokers for you.)
- **Webull:** `www.webull.com`

4

Bitcoin Investing

Why do people own Bitcoin? For the great majority, the answer is simple: *to make money!* But Bitcoin — for the moment, at least — is not a true currency. Sure, you *can* buy things with it, if you go out of your way to do so, but *why?* There are far more convenient ways to buy your groceries or pay for a night at the movies. If you think Bitcoin will go up in value, it makes sense to own some, but if you think Bitcoin will go up in value, then why would you buy coffee with it? If you think Bitcoin will go *down* in value, then why would you own it just for the *inconvenience* of buying stuff with it?

No, the vast majority of people who own Bitcoin do so because they believe that it will appreciate in value and multiply their wealth. In fact, Bitcoin is really an *asset,* not a currency. Even the Internal Revenue Service (IRS) in the United States has ruled that it should be treated as an asset for tax purposes, like gold or art.

There are, of course, others — those we call the true believers — who really do *believe* in Bitcoin. These folks think Bitcoin is the future of money, that if it's not a currency now, it will be one day, and they often also believe that Bitcoin is the beginning of a new and better world in which governments do not control money. But let's be frank: Whatever their beliefs, they also want to make money!

Isn't that why *you*, dear reader, are reading these very words right now? Yes, it is, so in this chapter we talk about investing in Bitcoin — what it is and how to get it.

TIP

We don't pretend to be seers. The following information is based on observations of the cryptocurrency markets over the last few years. As you'll see as you read through this chapter, we've tried to be cautious. We've explained, for instance, what other people have done, which doesn't mean we're saying that you should do the same! We strongly recommend that before you invest more than "play money" in Bitcoin or other cryptocurrencies, you further your education in the Bitcoin and cryptocurrency field and make up your own mind about what investing strategies might make sense for you.

What Bitcoin Actually Is

So, what is Bitcoin? Well, we can tell you what it isn't very quickly. It's not tangible — there's nothing you can touch or hold. You can't taste it or smell it. You can't even see it. In fact, Bitcoin really *isn't*. In other words, *there is no Bitcoin.*

What there is, though, is something known as the Bitcoin *ledger* (another word, by the way, that Satoshi Nakamoto didn't use in his famous Bitcoin white paper, but that is what the data stored in the Bitcoin blockchain has come to be popularly known as). A ledger is a written record of transactions; your checkbook's little account register is a form of ledger, for instance. (For those of you under 30, a check is a piece of paper you can write a number on, sign your name, and give to someone, and that someone can then give it to their bank and the bank gives them money — an amazingly efficient system.) Or consider a bank statement, showing money coming into and leaving your account (all too often *leaving*). That's a form of ledger, too.

So, when Satoshi Nakamoto created the first ever Bitcoin, how did he create it? Well, when we talk about Bitcoin being "created," we're really talking in shorthand. No Bitcoin *thing* was created. When Nakamoto first "created" Bitcoin, what he really did was to create a set of rules for a ledger in which he *recorded* the creation of Bitcoin. The ledger says, in effect,

"50 new Bitcoin were created today." And there you go, Bitcoin exists.

When Nakamoto minted that first "genesis block," the nature of the network was set in computational stone. Buried in the first block of data was a little additional text, words from the front page of that day's *New York Times* (January 3, 2009): "Chancellor on Brink of Second Bailout for Banks." Perhaps this was a hint at Nakamoto's reason for creating the network, as an alternative to what he felt were the corrupt government-managed monetary systems.

TIP The ledger essentially records two things.

- The first is the creation of Bitcoin, which is done through a process called *mining*. Nakamoto "mined" those original 50 Bitcoins (however, the first 50 Bitcoins are unspendable due to the nature of the code). Mining continues, and in fact, new Bitcoins are created each time a new block of transactions is added to the Bitcoin blockchain, every ten minutes or so.

  However, there is a mathematical arrangement to all this: Bitcoins are created on a steady schedule, and every four years or so (during an event quaintly called the *halvening*), the number of Bitcoins created every ten minutes is halved. Right now, 6.25 Bitcoins are created every ten minutes, but sometime in 2024, that will be reduced to 3.125, then again halved four years later, and so on (every four years) until around the year 2140, when the maximum number of Bitcoins will finally be in circulation.

- The second thing that the ledger records is what happens to the Bitcoin once it has been created. All Bitcoin is associated with "addresses" in the blockchain, and as people buy and sell Bitcoin, or use Bitcoin to buy something (essentially the same as selling Bitcoin), the coins get sent from one address in the blockchain to another. The Bitcoin ledger keeps track of where the Bitcoin flows, from address to address to address. Each address is under the control of someone; thus, the blockchain is, in effect, keeping track of who owns what. If the Bitcoin blockchain ledger says the address you control has 2 Bitcoins associated with it, then you control those 2 Bitcoins.

Bitcoin Units

To begin with, you need to understand that Bitcoin can be broken down and bought and sold in pieces. A Bitcoin is not like a gold coin; if you buy, for instance, a collectible coin from the Royal Canadian Mint, you're buying the whole thing. You're not buying half or a quarter.

But with Bitcoin, which can sell for tens of thousands of dollars *per coin*, most people couldn't afford to buy in if they had to buy the entire thing. And in any case, there is no physical coin — it's just an entry in the ledger.

So, that entry in the ledger can say whatever we want it to say. It can say that you bought half a Bitcoin, or a tenth or a hundredth or a ten thousandth, all the way to a single one hundred millionth. That is, you can buy partial coins — fragments of a Bitcoin. Table 4-1 offers a quick look at Bitcoin units.

Unit	Unit Name
1 (one)	Bitcoin, BTC, ₿
1/10 (one tenth)	deci-Bitcoin, dBTC
1/1,000 (one thousandth)	milli-Bitcoin, millibit
1/1,000,000 (one millionth)	micro-Bitcoin, μBTC, bit
1/100,000,000 (one hundred millionth)	Satoshi, sat

Table 4-1: *Bitcoin Units*

The table doesn't show all the units, but these are the units you're most likely to see and hear about. Because Bitcoins are divided into Satoshis — one hundred million Satoshis in each Bitcoin — you can divide a Bitcoin into tenths: deci-Bitcoin, centi-Bitcoin, milli-Bitcoin, micro-Bitcoin, and so on. (In fact, there is even a theoretical way to divide a Bitcoin down below the Satoshi level into *milliSatoshi,* using a special ancillary network called the Lightning Network.)

Is there enough of the smallest Bitcoin unit to go around? Well, take a look. There will only ever be 21 million Bitcoins; that means there will only ever be, at its maximum, 2,100,000,000,000,000 Satoshis in circulation.

Today, though, around 19 million Bitcoins are in circulation, and somewhere around 1,900,000,000,000,000 Satoshis.

TIP With around eight billion folks living on the planet, today, about 230,000 Satoshis are in circulation per person (the number fluctuates; see the Satoshi clock at `https://satoshisperperson.com`). Today, that's valued at around US$87 or C$111.

TIP All this means is that you don't need a huge sum of money to get started with Bitcoin. You can buy small pieces of a Bitcoin, but beware the fees. Buying small quantities at a traditional exchange can be expensive; in some cases, you'll likely be paying more in fees than the price of the Bitcoin. Some exchange sites now have fee-free transactions (see, for instance, Strike [`https://strike.me`]).

Bitcoin: Valuable Asset or Bubble about to Burst?

The decision on whether to invest in Bitcoin really comes down to one thing: Do you believe Bitcoin will continue to rise in value? Of course, that's true for any asset you might buy as an investment. The difference between Bitcoin and other assets is that the other assets have a track record — years, even hundreds or thousands of years, of fluctuations in value — while Bitcoin is so new that nobody can say for sure what will happen.

Bitcoin is what is often known as a *store of value*. That is, you can use it to store your wealth, and then retrieve that wealth at a later date. There's no question that Bitcoin is a store of value right now, though an unstable one. The questions are, though, will it continue to be a store of value, and will it go up in value?

This debate has smart people on both sides. Some intelligent, educated people believe that Bitcoin will inevitably increase in value, and some intelligent, educated people are just as sure that it will eventually collapse. We're in uncharted territory with no long-term history to point to or learn from; these are all projections.

The following sections lay out reasons for why Bitcoin is bound to continue rising in value and why it's bound to collapse.

Bitcoin's got to rise in value!

TIP

We begin with several reasons showing why Bitcoin's value will increase:

- **The Bitcoin market is currently worth almost a trillion dollars.** That represents millions of people who are already believers, who are not likely to cut and run. They want — and expect — the Bitcoin market to continue.
- **More money is flooding into Bitcoin from billionaires.** A few examples are Elon Musk (of Tesla), Jack Dorsey (of Twitter), Michael Saylor (of MicroStrategy), and the Winklevoss twins (of Facebook fame — who admittedly became billionaires because of their Bitcoin investments). A lot of wealthy people believe in Bitcoin.
- **As an asset, Bitcoin has a lot of advantages.** It's highly portable, far more portable than gold, the closest tangible asset to Bitcoin. It's also international, allowing people around the world to easily transfer money between nations.
- **Gold doesn't have much intrinsic value, and yet it has endured as a store of value for thousands of years.** Even crypto-skeptic economist Paul Krugman concedes that Bitcoin may endure, too, for the same reasons that gold has.

- **The Global Chief Economist at Citigroup once called gold a "6,000-year bubble" and even "shiny Bitcoin."** If gold can last, without much intrinsic value, for 6,000 years, can't Bitcoin (let's call it "weightless gold") survive for a while at least?
- **Bitcoin is very attractive to citizens of countries with problem currencies.** For example, citizens of Turkey, Venezuela, Zimbabwe, and other countries can buy into an asset that's far more stable (as volatile as it is) than their nations' currencies.
- **Bitcoin is very attractive to people fleeing their homelands.** It's a refugee's perfect asset, safer and more convenient than cash, jewelry, diamonds, or gold when escaping one's nation. Afghanistan, for instance, has recently become a Bitcoin hot spot.
- **Major financial institutions are getting into Bitcoin.** You can buy Bitcoin from the Cash App, PayPal, Robinhood, Venmo, and so on.

In economic terms, *intrinsic value* refers to an asset's value that's not related to its market value. Intrinsic value refers to the objective value an object has due to its intrinsic properties, not the value assigned to it by an investment market. Gold, for instance, is valuable because it's regarded as a store of value. But what if it *wasn't* regarded as a store of value? What if its only value was related to its industrial uses? Then its value —

its intrinsic value — would be far less, a fraction of its current market value.

The fact that Bitcoin has no intrinsic value doesn't really seem particularly relevant to us. After all, many stores of value have little or no intrinsic value: gold, art, baseball cards. A store of value doesn't need to have intrinsic value to be a store of value. It needs to be in short supply relative to demand, with no way for anyone to flood the market with new supply.

Bitcoin's bound to bust!

On the flip side of the Bitcoin, here are several reasons foretelling its doom:

- **Bitcoin has some significant disadvantages.** Either it's easy to use (but also easy to lose — perhaps as many as 20 percent of all Bitcoin has already been lost), or it's very secure but very complicated.
- **Bitcoin has no intrinsic value.** Thus, in the words of economist Paul Krugman, it isn't tethered to the real economy.
- **Bitcoin is used for illicit transactions.** Examples include funding terrorism, the drug trade, gun sales, money laundering, and so on. It follows that such transactions will lead to Bitcoin coming under more government scrutiny.

- **Bitcoin uses obscene amounts of electricity.** It takes a lot to keep the network running and the miners mining.
- **Bitcoin processes transactions too slowly.** It can take minutes to process a transaction, whereas the Visa network, for example, processes tens of thousands of transactions *per second.*
- **Bitcoin is simply too volatile to last.** Its volatility is an indicator that it isn't fully trusted.
- **Bitcoin is not backed by anything.** It's not backed by governments, by gold, by anything.
- **Scarcity itself is not a source of value.** Bitcoiners often point to its scarcity as being important, and in response critics say, in effect, "Scarcity isn't enough. There has to be something more!"
- **Bitcoin is a "fraud."** At least, according to Jamie Dimon, CEO of JPMorgan Chase, it is.

TIP Many of the complaints about Bitcoin are actually due to a misunderstanding about the nature of the beast:

- Illicit transactions? Isn't cash used for those, too?
- It's not backed by anything? It's backed by the millions of people who believe in it, just as gold is.
- It processes transactions too slowly? It processes transactions plenty fast enough to act as a tradeable

asset, and developments are under way to make it fast enough to work as a currency (if anyone really cares about that).

- Too volatile? Have you looked at the gold market recently? Plus, so what if it's volatile? Bitcoin has performed better than gold over the past few years, even *with* its volatility.

Oh, and about Jamie Dimon. He may not have changed his personal views, but JPMorgan Chase actually created its own cryptocurrency, JPM Coin, and recently provided access for its investors to six cryptocurrency funds.

And about the idea that scarcity is not a source of value: Consider the comments made by Professor Eswar Prasad, the author of a book about the future of money (titled *The Future of Money*) in the *New York Times* (June 14, 2021). He points out that Bitcoin has no intrinsic value and then responds to the claim by "Bitcoin devotees" that its value comes from scarcity, by saying: "Scarcity by itself can hardly be a source of value. Bitcoin investors seem to be relying on the greater fool theory — all you need to profit from an investment is to find someone willing to buy the asset at an even higher price."

But can't the same be said about gold? It has very little intrinsic value. It has only been valuable for the last 6,000 years because there's always been someone (another fool?) willing to buy the otherwise worthless metal, often at a higher price.

So, You Want to Buy Bitcoin

Let's say you come down on the side of Bitcoin continuing its rise; you want to join the crowd and buy in. You have a few basic questions to consider before you begin:

- Are you buying at a reasonable price?
- Can you keep your Bitcoin safe?
- Are you overinvesting?

First, understand how to buy Bitcoin at the best price, though you should balance this with security. Sometimes Bitcoin is "cheap" for a reason (you're being scammed, for instance!). You also need to really understand how to keep your Bitcoin safe. You don't want to be one of the thousands of people who've had their Bitcoin stolen or simply lost access to it.

And then you have to ask the perennial investing question: Are you risking too much? What if you're wrong, and Bitcoin doesn't survive?

TIP Don't invest more than you can afford to lose (or that you can stomach losing).

Be very careful you don't get caught up in FOMO — fear of missing out. Yes, if you'd taken all your savings early in 2016 and put them *all* into Bitcoin, you would have multiplied your money 40 times (at the time of writing; maybe *more* by the time you read this). But that was then — there's no going back. Millions of people in the history of the world have ruined themselves financially by taking the big bet and losing.

Investing in Bitcoin is definitely a bet. Don't get too greedy. Invest a sum that won't ruin you if the naysayers prove to be right, a sum that you can shrug off if necessary. Perhaps you shrug it off after a period of anguish, but you shrug it off (at least eventually!).

The basic strategy: Buy and hodl

Here's the primary strategy for investing in Bitcoin:

1. **Buy Bitcoin.**
2. **Hold it.**
3. **Wait for it to go up in price.**
4. **Keep holding it because it will probably go up more.**

This might be termed a *hodling strategy.* And perhaps this sounds very simplistic, but it really is the primary investment strategy, and many people have become very rich using this strategy.

TIP Okay, so it's a bit of Bitcoin jargon, a cryptocurrency joke. Instead of "holding" your Bitcoin, you — in Bitcoin parlance — *hodl* it. It all comes from a message posted in the Bitcoin talk forums (`https://bitcointalk.org`) in 2013, from a forum member named GameKyuubi, explaining (reportedly while drunk) that he couldn't figure out the ups and downs of Bitcoin and, thus, intended to simply hold (mistyped *hodl*) his Bitcoin for the long term. The long term has been good to GameKyuubi, if indeed he did hold long term. He created a widely used term in the Bitcoin community, and his Bitcoin went from an exchange rate of $716 per Bitcoin down to $438 and then, over the years, up to a peak (so far, at the time of this writing) of almost $64,000.

Let's take a look at the price of Bitcoin over time. We'll use information from CoinMarketCap (`https://coinmarketcap.com`), a great site for checking the pricing of a huge selection of cryptocurrencies. Consider the rise and fall of Bitcoin between the start of 2016 and the end of 2021. At the start of 2016, the price was $433 per Bitcoin; at the end of 2021, the price was $46,727. The peak was almost $67,000.

Yes, Bitcoin pricing has a lot of volatility; it's a wild ride. But a hodl strategy from 2016 would have worked extremely well. You'd be entering 2022 having increased your investment around 50 to 60 times. Even if you had bought at the peak in 2017 (when Bitcoin really came to the attention of the masses) and then continued hodling during the precipitous decline in early 2018, you'd still be way ahead. You'd have more than doubled your money.

Dollar cost averaging

Dollar cost averaging (DCA) is a popular strategy in the Bitcoin field, and it's an investing concept that's been around for a long time. It's related to investing in traditional investment vehicles or assets such as mutual funds.

The idea is that you invest a set sum on a regular basis — every week or month, for instance. You don't pay much attention to the price at any point; you simply invest that sum every period. When the price is high, you'll be buying less of the asset; when the price is low, you'll be buying more.

TIP

The purpose of DCA is to keep you investing in an asset that has a history of rising in value over time, without the risk of trying to time the market with a large lump sum and getting it wrong. You don't think about the investment; you just do it each time it's scheduled.

So, many people dollar cost average into Bitcoin. For instance, you might decide you want to invest $1,000 in Bitcoin this year. (Let's call it $1,040 to make the math easy.) You set up an auto-purchase at an exchange to invest $20 every Friday, so you spread your $1,040 over 52 weeks.

You can see this at work using a DCA calculator such as dcaBTC (`https://dcabtc.com`) or the one at `www.bitcoindollarcostaverage.com`. What would've happened if you'd invested US$20 a week starting three years ago, as shown in the dcaBTC calculator? According to this calculator, you would have invested US$3,140; at the current value of Bitcoin, you'd own US$14,550 worth. (US$3,140 at US$20 a week is actually three years and one week for some reason. We're not saying these calculators are highly accurate, but they give an idea of what's going on.)

TIP: Here are a couple of things to understand about DCA:

- **It doesn't protect you from losses when you invest in a highly speculative asset that collapses in value.** It's an investment strategy that works well to give people the discipline to invest in an asset that's known to rise over time, despite periodic drops in value. Bitcoin definitely has periodic drops in value and definitely has, to date, risen over time. Will it continue to do so? That's a decision you have to make, whether you believe it will or not.
- **If you're sure the asset will rise over the long term, then a lump sum invested early might drop in value over the short term — but over the long term it might provide much higher returns than DCA.** Had you

invested three years' worth of weekly $20 periodic investments ($3,120) at the *beginning* of the three-year period, the value would now be more than $30,000. But again, market timing is very difficult, and we don't know what's going to happen over the *next* three years.

Timing the market

If you can figure out how to time the market, you can make much more money. Let's say you invested $1,000 into Bitcoin in February 2017 when it was $1,000 a coin, and then:

1. You held it until late in 2017 and sold it when it peaked. Your $1,000 is now about $19,000.
2. You cleverly held it until the price bottomed out and bought again at around $3,400 at the end of 2018. Your 1 Bitcoin is now around 5.5 Bitcoins.
3. You knew there would be another peak, so you watched carefully. In April 2021, you sold your 5.5 Bitcoins for $349,000. In four years, you increased your investment 349 times.

Simple! *That's* the way to get rich: Time the market! Keep in mind, though, if you screw up your timing, it won't work so well. Is timing the market possible? Plenty of people will tell you it is — all sorts of Bitcoin prognosticators, who have all sorts of theories.

Consider, for instance, Über Holger's Bitcoin Rainbow. The idea is that Bitcoin is on a long-term upward curve, but with fluctuations. It's like a rainbow curving up into the sky, but sometimes the price of Bitcoin is at the bottom edge of the rainbow; other times, near the top.

The closer the price is to the upper edge of the rainbow, the stronger the signal to sell; the closer it is to the lower edge, the stronger the signal to buy.

There are a couple of things to consider with this model. If you just hodl, you'll make money anyway. The rainbow is on an upward curve, remember! Plus, well, we'll let Mr. Holger tell you. The Bitcoin Rainbow is not intended as investment advice, and as you've no doubt heard many times, past performance is not an indication of future results. As he explains: "The Rainbow Chart is meant to be a fun way of looking at long-term price movements, disregarding the daily volatility 'noise.' The color bands follow a logarithmic regression (introduced by Bitcoin Talk user trololo in 2014), but are otherwise completely arbitrary and without any scientific basis. It will only be correct until one day it isn't anymore."

You can find plenty of market-timing advice if that's what you want; we'll let you seek it out. Just be aware that timing markets is very difficult to get right and quite easy to get wrong.

Arbitrage

Another investment technique some people use is *arbitrage*. The term means "the simultaneous buying and selling of securities, currency, or commodities in different markets or in derivative forms in order to take advantage of differing prices for the same asset" (see www.lexico.com/en/definition/arbitrage).

Here's a simple example: Suppose a kid used to be in the toy arbitrage business. He would visit toy stores looking for products on sale at a deep discount, check their prices at Amazon using his smartphone, and if the price disparity was enough, he'd buy them, ship them to Amazon, and sell them through Amazon's third-party seller program. He was looking for price disparities in two different marketplaces and taking advantage of them.

The principle's the same with Bitcoin. In this case, you're taking advantage of pricing that differs across exchanges. (However, it's probably closer between exchanges these days than in the past.) The goal is to find a big enough difference between two exchanges to make it worthwhile to buy on one and then sell on the other.

There are, of course, problems with this. Often the differences are very slim on the more reputable exchanges. There's often a fraction-of-a-percent difference — a 1 percent difference is often a big deal — so you'll need to trade a lot of Bitcoin to make much money. You have to consider exchange fees and transaction fees, and you should also beware of rapid price fluctuations that can ruin your move within seconds.

Still, some people play these games and are even involved in "triangular" arbitrage. This is when you start with Bitcoin, trade it for another, undervalued, cryptocurrency, and then trade that for something else. Then you trade the last cryptocurrency to get back to Bitcoin, with a little more than you started with. Arbitrage "bots" can automate the process. But we're not going into any more detail. If you really want to play this game, first do some serious research and get all your ducks in a row.

Other Bitcoin-related investment vehicles

You have other ways to invest in the Bitcoin revolution, some without even buying Bitcoin itself. You might want to invest in the picks and shovels.

The concept of *picks-and-shovels investing* is the idea of investing not directly into a new industry, but in the companies that support that industry. The name refers to the North American gold rushes of the 19th century. While most people rushed to the gold fields to mine for gold, many people decided instead to support the miners by, for instance, operating bars, restaurants, and hotels, and selling supplies (the picks and shovels). Many got rich doing so (with far less effort and risk than mining gold).

TIP

You'll find numerous investing opportunities in the picks and shovels of the Bitcoin revolution:

- Bitcoin exchanges, such as Coinbase (COIN) and Kraken.
- Cryptocurrency mining companies, some of which have gone public, such as Riot Blockchain (RIOT), Hive Blockchain Technologies (HIVE), and Marathon Digital Holdings (MARA).
- Companies making mining equipment, such as Canaan (CAN).
- Exchange-traded funds (ETFs; see Chapter 2), which are funds traded on a stock exchange like an actual company stock but are funds that invest in particular types of investments or a particular market. Some ETFs now invest in Bitcoin and other cryptocurrencies. Grayscale (`www.grayscale.com`), for instance, has a variety of cryptocurrency funds, including the Bitcoin Trust.

Hodling II: An Even Better Strategy

The big hodling gains in the Bitcoin market, of course, went to people who bought well before the big appreciation of 2017.

These people were well ahead of the game, buying, mining, and hodling Bitcoin in 2015, 2014, or earlier.

Consider Satashi Nakamoto, who created around a million Bitcoin starting in 2009. Multiply one million by US$38,000, the approximate price as we write these words. (We'll save you time: It's 38 billion U.S. dollars, or more than 48.5 billion Canadian dollars.) And then consider that he created this Bitcoin *out of thin air* at a time when it had essentially *no value*. It cost essentially nothing more than a little electricity to run a personal computer. (Don't get excited; mining no longer takes "nothing more than a little electricity." It now takes a major investment in electricity.)

This is an important concept, so bear with us a moment. Here's an even better hodling strategy than the one we described earlier:

1. Build a time machine.
2. Go back to 2009.
3. Buy or mine Bitcoin (in vast quantities).
4. Hold it.
5. Wait for it to go up in price.
6. Sell it. (Just how much money do you need?)

This may sound trite, but it's a really important concept because you have to understand that the really big Bitcoin gains are over!

Stories of huge profits have, to a great degree, generated the interest in Bitcoin that led you to this chapter. There are people who bought or mined Bitcoin at a price of, say, $1. Those Bitcoins have multiplied in value 38,000 times! (We're using a starting price of $1 because we don't know how to divide $0 into $38,000.) That simply cannot happen again. Dramatic stories like these have generated such a huge interest, but it's simply not realistic to believe the entire stock of Bitcoin will one day be worth $48,000,000,000,000,000 or so (somewhere around 500 times the world's gross domestic product).

TIP

That's not to say that Bitcoin can't still double, triple, or quintuple in price, or even much more. But it does mean that if you're looking for greater profits, if you're looking for 20 times or 50 times in the short term, you have to look elsewhere.

5
The Fintech Landscape

Fintech has undoubtedly become one of the hottest topics in business. Web searches for the term *fintech* in Google have grown exponentially in the last several years, so it's obvious that people are curious about it. But what is it, and why is it relevant to today's financial industry? This chapter looks at those very basic questions.

Globally, the fintech market is booming, and investors are participating across all stages of fintech companies' life cycles. Many banks are investing strategically in fintech companies to hedge themselves from disruption, but many are also collaborating with fintech firms to gain a win-win situation.

Venture capital (VC) firms are in search of the most distinctive fintech companies that can become the next disruptors to the current banking norm. Private equity (PE) firms are looking for the company that can roll up many "diamonds in the rough" to create a large and significant multibillion-dollar market-cap company. The winners and losers will help define the financial industry for decades to come.

Investing in fintech firms can be like playing a game of chance, but there are ways to increase your odds of winning. This is essentially what VCs and PEs do every day. They try to run their winners and mitigate against risk to improve their returns. Of course, each fintech start-up wants to take the smart money, and the smart money wants companies that have viable business plans and the credibility or pedigrees to build sustainable, profitable businesses.

In this chapter, we explain who is investing, how to identify future rising fintech stars, and how to compete against the most well-known VCs and PEs in the industry. You get the steps necessary to find the correct fintech investment vehicles and to perform due diligence so the odds are in your favor.

What Is Fintech, Anyway?

TIP There are many definitions of *fintech*, but for the purposes of this chapter, this one is the most relevant: Fintech companies are businesses that leverage new technology to create better financial services for both consumers and businesses. Of course, that begs

> another question: What is *financial technology?* We define it as all parts of technology that help provide financial services and products to customers. Those customers can be individuals, companies, or governments.

Fintech is also frequently used as an umbrella term for various subcategories, such as *wealthtech* and *regtech*. Here's a quick summary of them:

- **Capital markets tech,** in which companies leverage newer technology such as artificial intelligence (AI), machine learning, and blockchain, is led by seasoned capital markets veterans and is both collaborating with and disrupting the financial services incumbents.
- **Wealthtech** unites wealth and technology to provide digital tools for personal and professional wealth management and investing. This sector includes brokerage platforms, automated/semiautomated robo-advisors, and self-directed investment tools for individual investors and advisors to navigate the changing landscape in wealth management.
- **Insurtech** is a combination of insurance and technology. It refers to innovations that generate efficiency and cost savings from the existing insurance industry model.
- **Regtech** is a community of technology companies that solve regulatory challenges through automation. The

increase in major regulatory policy and the rise in digital products have made it imperative for companies to check for and implement compliance issues, and this can be difficult with old, manual processes.

- **Paytech** refers to the combination of payments and technology. Innovative payment services now form part of the paytech ecosystem and have dominated the early days of the fintech revolution through mobile, cross-border, peer-to-peer, and cryptocurrency payments. Financial institutions have had to digitize their current offerings to create new channels linked to a digital platform.
- **AI in finance** refers to how AI, machine learning, and deep learning are applied across financial services companies today and how they could be used in the future.
- **Legaltech** combines the nature of legal technologies and their relationship with data, the Internet of Things (IOT), cybersecurity, and distributed ledger technologies, as well as ethical considerations of the technological advancement.

A Few Important Fintech Terms

As you dive into the world of fintech, you find many terms to describe the various parts of the industry and its inner (and outer!) workings. To get started, here's a core set of definitions that it may help to have in your back pocket at the outset:

- An *application programming interface* (API) is a software intermediary that enables two applications to talk to each other. It delivers your message request to a provider and then delivers the response back to you.

  To better understand APIs, imagine that you had friends over, and you wanted to serve an Italian dinner. You could assemble all the ingredients yourself and make it, but it would take an hour and a half, and you have only 30 minutes. What do you do? You pull out a jar of spaghetti sauce, boil some water for dried pasta, and buy a prepared loaf of garlic bread. And voilà! Dinner is served.

  TIP Having APIs in your programming pantry is like having premade spaghetti sauce, garlic bread, and pasta. The components/ingredients needed to prepare the program are all available in the source code. When bundled together, they make up the API.

- *Data management* means collecting, cleansing, managing, and analyzing data to generate additional business intelligence.
- A *decentralized application* (DApp) stores data in a decentralized database and uses decentralized computing

resources in a peer-to-peer network. This open-source code can be accessed by all network members.

- *Digital transformation* is the change that happens to a business when you apply and integrate digital technology. It includes changes to business processes, business models, domain expertise, technology, and culture.
- *Disruption* refers to the way emerging fintech firms and technologies are interfering or competing with the traditional way business has been done in the past.
- *Microservices* is an approach to application development in which a large application is built as a set of modular components. In other words, as the name implies, they're small, reusable services that work together, like the APIs you find out about earlier in this chapter. Each microservice is independently maintained and represented by individual APIs.
- *Open source* is software for which the source code is freely available to anyone. Any capable programmers can then use, modify, and distribute their own versions of the program. Nobody creating or modifying the code receives any direct compensation. Programmers are motivated by a desire to improve and augment the initial package, and the result is a better functioning and more highly interactive software.

Some people use the term *open source* interchangeably with *free software,* but they're not the same thing. Free software is a philosophical position around the use and ownership of code, whereas open source is a methodology around the use of public code.

The Fintech Players

When deciding whether to invest in the fintech space, you need to consider the differences between consumer-driven investments (for example, the company that makes your favorite mobile finance app) and corporate-driven fintech investments (for example, the company that makes the internal software a bank uses to manage customer accounts):

- In the business-to-consumer (B2C) arena, some fintech companies strive to disrupt the industry by providing new financial apps directly to consumers. These apps are appealing because they're easier, quicker, and cheaper to use than those that traditional financial institutions *(incumbents)* provide.
- The business-to-business (B2B) space focuses on fintech firms that are looking to collaborate with — rather than disrupt — existing institutions by providing products that increase their efficiency, flexibility, and profitability.

The incumbents, in turn, provide new products to their clients.

- There's also a middle ground, known as business-to-business-to-consumer (B2B2C). In B2B2C, fintech firms sell their offerings to incumbents, who then *white-label* (rebrand) each offering as their own and sell it to their clients. If you drive a car, you've experienced that yourself, because your car company hasn't manufactured all the parts. Instead, it purchases them from a supplier and assembles them (and you'd never know the name of the supplier). The same happens in banking today: Banks assemble lots of fintech solutions from fintech firms and put their own names and branding all over it.

How these entities may attempt to raise funding, and how they deploy their funding, can be very different. Understanding the differentiation between these types of entities, therefore, will help you as you explore your investment options and decide where to put your money.

TIP

The world of investors and investing is changing as a result of the fintech revolution; this area of fintech applied to the global investment management sector is called wealthtech. For more information, check out *The WealthTech Book* by Susanne Chishti and Thomas Puschmann (published by Wiley).

Challenging financial institutions

Some fintech firms are focused on disrupting the existing financial landscape, whereas others recognize that they need to collaborate with existing players to benefit from their size and distribution.

The fintech firms that provide technology services to consumers or retail clients (B2C), largely in the form of cellphone-based applications (apps), are more likely to act as challengers to financial institutions, because individuals can make the buying decision for those products themselves.

The types of B2C fintech apps and their functions are numerous. Initially, a number of apps arose around payment facilities (paytech). From there, foreign exchange was a natural segue for international transactions. This led to lending providers with more sophisticated credit scoring. More recently, fully fledged challenger banks have become popular, some of which are mobile-only enabled. Also, robo-advisory firms in the wealth management space and insurtech firms are competing for insurance underwriting.

These fintech firms are disrupting established financial institutions' higher-margin retail businesses. How sustainable these business models are in the long run remains to be seen, as well as whether there may be consolidation among some of them or they may be bought by the established players.

Offering collaborative solutions

The fintech firms that provide technology services to established financial institutions are more likely to act as collaborators with those institutions. They're largely based around workflow processes or making manual processes more efficient. Large financial institutions have historically spent hundreds of millions of dollars, if not billions, on technology that gives them an edge, improves compliance, or helps them cut costs.

However, as margins have reduced, interest rates have remained low, and capital adequacy requirements have increased, large institutions have become less inclined to continue to build all this themselves. They're looking for shared services.

Fintech firms enable institutions to focus on their core technology and look for best-of-breed offerings in technology areas where they don't need a competitive advantage. The adoption of this model is still relatively fledgling, but demand appears to be growing.

Fintech adoption challenges the cultural approach of a traditional organization and its ability to change, particularly when considered as part of a collaboration with established financial institutions. Fintech has also embraced cultural aspects from a wider society perspective. The "wall of money" that's expected to drown the investment market in the coming years is focused on environmental, social, and governance

(ESG) considerations (see Chapter 8 for an introduction to ESG investing). Companies are investigating how they can become more socially responsible from an ethical perspective but also remain competitive in an environment where consumers and investors are looking for reasons to support, or not, a given company.

Therefore, new fintech entrepreneurs are responding with products that promote cultural change, financial inclusion, and diversity. These resonate with some of the investors already described but have also unearthed new "impact" investors that are focused on corporate responsibility, as well as a return on investment (ROI).

Fintech Investment Vehicles

Where you sit in the investment hierarchy generally dictates what access you have to given investments and what your risk appetite may be. This is also true for the different investment vehicles in the fintech investor landscape. The following sections highlight some of the most common investment vehicles.

Crowdfunding

Crowdfunding is a way for individuals to collectively invest in a business in return for a potential profit or reward by responding to a pitch posted on a crowdfunding website. Crowdfunding can be very exciting for new investors, because they can back young, exciting start-ups and help them raise the money they need to grow. Often multiple banks will have rejected these early start-ups for loans, so these investments can be quite risky.

TIP Several types of crowdfunding exist:

- **Loan-based:** Peer-to-peer (P2P) lending is provided in return for a set interest rate (such as Lending Club and Funding Circle).
- **Reward-based:** Money is invested in return for non-monetary returns, typically samples of the product developed. This is the type of crowdfunding on sites like Kickstarter and Indiegogo.
- **Investment-based:** This entails receiving shares in return for your investment, which is what we focus on in this chapter.

Investment-based crowdfunding is more the norm in Europe (particularly in the United Kingdom with companies such as Crowdcube and Seedrs) and more recently Asia. Reward-based investment is more popular in the United States due to regulations around investor requirements, although the JOBS Act (May 2016) extended online equity crowdfunding opportunities in the United States.

The very nature of crowdfunding lends itself to B2C-type investments because individuals can relate more to a consumer-focused application (see the earlier section "The Fintech Players" for more information). The product being developed may be something they'd use themselves. So companies may raise a relatively small amount of money from hundreds or even thousands of investors, which in total gives them a decent funding round.

TIP Crowdfunding platforms will give you a choice of many companies that need money to grow. The most popular sites make it fun and enjoyable to browse these exciting companies and their products, making it easy for you to part with your money. However, you should never invest money you can't afford to lose because you may not get it back, and you should invest only in what you completely understand.

The amount of due diligence retail investors do is relatively light, given the funds invested. However, firms on such platforms have increased the amount of information they provide, giving a certain standardization around the type of investor presentations produced. The platforms also have an obligation to undertake a due diligence process before allowing companies to list on their sites. The crowdsourcing model is so new that good data isn't yet available to understand how the majority of the firms on such platforms perform from a return on investment (ROI) perspective.

Fewer B2B companies, particularly fintech companies, are available for investment on crowdfunding sites because B2B technologies aren't as immediately appealing to casual investors. A revolutionary new electronic gadget is just more "fun" to invest in than technology required for workflow processes within a financial institution. And that's why we need angel investors! Read on.

Angel investors

An *angel investor* is an accredited investor who provides financial backing, networking, business expertise, and other support to a small start-up in return for an equity share. Angel investors are typically sophisticated, experienced investors with high net worth and lots of readily available capital.

Angel investors are more likely to invest in businesses that are pre-revenue and seeking seed capital, because they tend to invest in businesses where they feel that they can add value through their domain expertise and network/contacts in that area. Therefore, angel investors generally take more risks than VC firms (covered in the next section), including investing their own money, and they invest more per company than individual crowdfunding investors do.

However, angels aren't just guardians. The majority are seasoned professionals who regularly take positions as nonexecutive directors within the firms that they invest in or provide advice and networking to further the firms' opportunities. In addition, many angels invest collectively as a group or syndicate, either within a given theme, such as fintech, or within random groups coming together under the guidance of one angel who acts as the lead investor.

In some European countries, particularly the United Kingdom, both crowd and angel investors receive income tax rebates/reliefs from their investments in start-up firms. This acts as an incentive for some investors to become more active in this space and improves the risk-reward ratio for such investors. In other countries, it's more common for the start-up companies themselves to receive tax rebates for their research and development investments.

Venture capital

VC firms do what angel investors do, but they do it on a corporate basis. Instead of investing their own money, venture capitalists (VCs) are paid to invest other people's money.

Managers of the venture funds, known as general partners (GPs), are typically investors who have years of experience investing and taking minority stakes in early stage firms. That's what they do for a living, unlike investors in crowdfunding sites or angel investors. GPs are good at investing (or else they lose their jobs).

VCs receive money from high-net-worth individuals, family offices, and corporations, all of which become limited partners (LPs) in the fund. Each of the LPs is looking for a diversified but higher return than what it can achieve from less risky investments, ordinarily for a fixed period of up to ten years. The GPs receive management fees (typically 2 percent of funds under management) to scout and invest in the right types of investments, conduct due diligence, and manage the resulting portfolio.

GPs and their firms typically take a carry fee (for example, 20 percent) of the performance of the fund (this management fee and performance fee are commonly referred to as "2 and 20"). The remainder of the profit (for example, 80 percent) is distributed to LPs. However, many funds have to achieve a *hurdle rate* (a return rate that investors must receive before the fund managers can receive their carry fee). For example, a fund's agreement may specify that the LPs must be paid back their invested capital, in addition to an agreed annual percentage yield, prior to the GP receiving their return.

To reduce the number of LPs that a fund services, a substantial minimum investment is typically required, putting such funds outside the scope of most regular investors. To invest in VCs, you must either be very rich or indirectly invest via a fund that serves as one of the LPs; this is called a *fund of funds* structure.

Because they're investing with other people's money, VCs tend to invest in businesses that are relatively established, with a given level of annual or monthly recurring revenue, at the Series A level of fundraising or later. Series A is generally the first funding round by VCs, Series B is the second funding round, Series C is the third funding round, and so on. Crowdfunding and angel investors are normally investing in seed or post-seed rounds that come before Series A.

Some VC firms are lately shifting their focus to later-stage investments (called *scale-up funding*), because the ROI for many funds has been lower than anticipated. Generally, VC investors should anticipate that about four out of ten firms will fail, and another four out of ten firms may return the monies invested. The remaining two firms would, therefore, need to have returns of ten times or more to achieve the type of returns expected. The very successful firms are called *unicorns*, a term that refers to start-up companies that achieve a $1 billion market valuation.

To protect their interests, VC firms are more likely to demand preference shares for their investment and receive veto or minority investor rights that aren't available to other investors. They also tend to act as the lead investor in a funding round, thereby dictating the valuation, total monies raised, and terms of the investment. Those terms may include the pre-money valuation of the firm, prior to investment, and the post-money valuation, which includes the funds raised added to the pre-money valuation. For example, a firm raising $1 million at a pre-money valuation of $10 million will have a post-money valuation of $11 million.

Corporate venture capital

As the name suggests, *corporate venture capital* (CVC) firms are like regular VC firms, but they invest on behalf of a given company. Their initial motive is, therefore, to invest in companies that will give some form of strategic benefit to the company, either immediately or in the future. As such, they tend to be focused on later-stage firms that can bring immediate revenue and/or profitability. Some CVCs also take outside money, where LPs invest alongside them. However, such funds may be split in focus between providing a good ROI to all investors and delivering a strategic benefit to the parent company.

For example, suppose that a bank has a corporate venture fund. It could decide to invest in a fintech company before it rolls out its fintech app to millions of consumers globally. The bank must decide whether it will immediately separate the funds made available as CVC or draw down funds from the bank's balance sheet to support the investment. (*Draw down* refers to collecting funds when an investment occurs, based on an agreement that such funds will be available when the CVC requests them.)

This decision can have a significant impact on the commitment to the investment, or at least the perception of commitment. The employees who manage the CVC aren't necessarily rewarded in the same way that a commercial VC would be, with respect to management and performance fees. Therefore, the incentives and, hence, the commitment can be questioned.

Good VC investors should make lots of money, because they share the performance fee. However, the manager running a CVC won't get such unlimited payments. Therefore, if someone is driven by money, they'd probably want to run their own VC fund. Having said that, in principle, CVCs should be better venture partners to fintech firms than regular VCs, because they have a competitive advantage due to their domain expertise, knowledge of markets, client networks, and technologies.

In addition, their stronger balance sheet makes them a more patient investor. They aren't looking only for mutual growth but also for more strategic benefits, such as direct synergies with their company's business that further drives additional revenue growth and valuation.

However, not all CVCs leverage these benefits. Internal stakeholders can question the start-up's ability to deliver or suggest that they can build the same thing themselves internally. Those that do succeed follow the mantra that "rip and replace" isn't the solution to managing old legacy systems and that "core and satellite" is a better strategy.

Of course, fintech firms need to consider whether a CVC minority investment gives them the necessary short-term capital injection to meet their scale-up aspirations in conjunction with the corporate "mother ship." They may find that aligning closely with one large corporate infrastructure reduces their ability to scale into other competing corporate infrastructures due to a paranoia around access to confidential data. In addition, the obvious exit may be full integration into the CVC's company, which may not give the same return as selling the product on the open market.

Private equity

Historically, PE funds have been viewed as more similar to the traditional asset managers of private investment. They tend to invest in much later-stage companies that already have substantial revenue and are, therefore, less risky investments. (Blackstone buying a majority stake in Refinitiv is a recent example.) Not many fintech firms are sufficiently large to qualify in that regard, so PE activity is more often found in other commercial sectors.

PEs have a similar structure to VCs, in that they involve GPs and LPs. However, the pools of capital raised for such funds tend to be much larger, as the company valuations of invested firms are much higher, given the firms' maturity, revenue, and profitability. PE funds typically have a fixed investment period, typically ranging from seven to ten years. There are similar management and performance fees (2 percent and 20 percent, respectively), although when institutional and ultra-high-net-worth individuals invest substantial funds, fees are often negotiable.

PE funds can also support investments such as leveraged buyouts, management buyouts, and company restructuring, whereby they regularly take majority or outright stakes in a company and use debt to finance large transactions, with the resulting burden of servicing that debt left with the company. They may then appoint management to make the company more profitable and valuable, which may include selling off pieces of the business in a "sum of the parts being greater than the whole" strategy. Alternatively, they may exit the investment through a trade sale to a strategic buyer (for example, Blackstone subsequently selling its stake in Refinitiv to the London Stock Exchange) or to another PE firm, or they may list the company on a stock exchange via an initial public offering (IPO).

How to Conduct Due Diligence

After you know the major types of investors (described earlier in this chapter), you can consider what firms these investors may be looking for and what assessment criteria they may use.

TIP It's important to do your own research to determine whether you're making a viable investment. This is true whether you're a private investor monitoring some crowdfunding opportunities or a portfolio manager at a large PE fund. The level of research will, of course, differ, but the principles are the same:

- Your initial primary research should focus on companies addressing the areas in which you're interested in investing. For example, you should decide whether you're interested in retail or corporate opportunities and whether you want to limit your search to a given business sector that you think has growth potential.

- Your secondary research should focus more deeply on individual companies. You'll need to determine whether there's a real market for their product, the size of the market opportunity, and the strength of the technology stack. Secondary research enables you to understand the business itself, its founders' credibility, and the potential of its offering.

The following sections look at the various types of research you may want to do in evaluating a potential fintech investment and how investors can analyze the data they gather.

Perform primary research

Primary research is all about finding investments that meet your criteria. So, of course, the first step of this process is to determine what your criteria actually are.

You may want to start by looking at where a company sits in the overall value chain: Is it B2C, B2B2C, or B2B focused? In other words, what is the general market sector the company targets? (See the earlier section "The Fintech Players" for more information.)

After you choose an overall sector, your next step is to determine whether to focus on a given vertical, such as wealth-tech or regtech, or on specific technology areas. Examples may include AI or blockchain. You could also go for a combination of two or more technology elements.

Then you must decide on the size and current success of the firm:

- Crowdfunding or angel investors may be happy to invest in seed-stage companies that are pre-revenue but may require the firms to be eligible for certain tax benefits, preferably available to the investor.
- VC, PE, and CVC normally require a minimum level of annual recurring revenue and/or number of employees, which can indicate the company is relatively established and on a growth trajectory that suggests it can scale up.

There is a wide universe of fintech firms out there, so a general Internet search is certainly not the most efficient way of identifying the right companies. Review the following list of research sources instead:

- **Databases:** For later-stage firms that have raised funds already, look in databases provided by firms such as Crunchbase (`www.crunchbase.com`) or PitchBook (`https://pitchbook.com`). These databases tell how much a firm has raised to date and which investors were part of those rounds. A certain bank investing in the firm suggests that the bank will also be using its product.

- **Accelerator programs:** For earlier-stage start-ups, sourcing accelerator programs such as Accenture's FinTech Innovation Lab (`www.fintechinnovationlab.com`) or Techstars (`www.techstars.com`) can be useful. These programs can help you find firms that have already been pre-vetted as part of the process to get into the program.
- **Incubators:** Incubator programs can help you find companies that have structured programs to help firms grow within the given vertical/technology being considered.
- **Associations:** Look at trade associations such as the Investment Association (`www.theiaengine.com`) or quasi-government-led initiatives such as Innovate Finance (`www.innovatefinance.com`). Platforms such as FINTECH Circle (`https://fintechcircle.com`) also offer custom scouting services for financial players to scout for the most relevant fintech companies.
- **Awards lists:** The top fintech companies in given sectors or regions are highlighted in various awards lists as some of the rising stars in the fintech world. If a firm appears among the award winners for several years, and across different awards providers, they'll have

shown their worth on multiple occasions. Generally, awards also have an element of vetting, because an industry panel will have nominated and/or voted for the most relevant firms.

Do secondary research

After you've identified some firms of interest, it's time to perform your own due diligence to ensure that the firms meet your requirements. Here's a general checklist to use as your starting point:

- Are they producing a real solution to a given problem, or are they producing a technology solution that is *looking* for a problem?
- Is the technology solution sufficiently differentiated from existing solutions, or does it create more efficiency and/or revenue?
- What is the differentiating business model, and how sustainable is it?
- What regulatory requirements, if any, does the business need to meet? Are there licenses or approvals to obtain?
- What is the addressable market for the solution? Is a small percentage of that market still sufficiently interesting to make the solution viable?

- Where is the current or likely competition for the solution? Does the fintech firm have a sufficiently superior approach to differentiate it from the competition?
- Is the product more likely to disrupt or collaborate with existing financial institutions' offerings? Are the founders clear on their direction?
- What is the sales approach for the solution, and what challenges does that provide? For example, for B2C, how critical is search engine optimization (SEO)? For B2B, what is the sales cycle length required for larger financial institutions?
- What is the current traction in terms of existing sales and potential pipeline?
- What are the current projected revenues and related cost structure that create the expected burn rate and associated runway for the business?

  The *burn rate* for a company is the regular monthly spend required to keep the firm in business. The *runway* is the length of time that a company can survive before needing more funding. Runway is determined by dividing the current funding available to the firm by the regular monthly spend. Of course, some firms start reducing their costs as they get closer to the end of their runway, to leave further time for revenue or funding opportunities.

- Who is on the team? What credibility and/or experience and network do they have? Do they have the right personalities or chemistry? Have they worked together before?
- For some investors, the team is the most important factor, superseding all other analysis. The company may have a great product, but if the team isn't aligned, or if the chemistry is wrong because their respective ambitions or drive don't fit, they may not be able to reach their goals collectively. Founder issues occur surprisingly frequently, perhaps driven by the stress of meeting short-term objectives with limited resources. Looking for those who have worked successfully together in the past can be a key indicator. In addition, understanding the founders' home life challenges and ability to support themselves while bootstrapping the company — that is, building the company from the ground up with nothing but personal savings — can help you assess the overall situation.
- What is the anticipated valuation of the business, pre-money and post-money? What amount of funding is required for what time frame to fund the business to the next milestones or funding requirement?
- What is the longer-term exit plan for the business? For example, do the founders hope for a trade sale or an IPO?

Analyze data

Some investors can take all or some of the primary and secondary market indicators and use them to scientifically score firms and build up an objective matrix to evaluate the right firms to invest in.

Other firms focus more on diversification. They calculate the optimal number of firms to give certain return levels, and those calculations may drive them to diversify across industry verticals, types of technology, thematics, and even geographic regions to achieve a blended portfolio that will give the greatest ROI with the lowest risk profile.

Some firms have built a business around objectively scoring investments based on the secondary market research factors, and investors will pay for such scorecards to simplify their due diligence process.

In addition, some investment platforms have enabled machine learning algorithms to matchmake certain fintech firms with established serial investors in that vertical or theme, alerting investors to firms that are looking to raise funds.

AI/machine learning factors are frequently applied at this stage to establish a scientific approach. However, personalities and leaders can also be a key element to success with some firms, and those things are more difficult to quantify.

How to Evaluate a Firm's Growth Strategies

When considering which fintech firms to invest in, it's important to understand a company's growth strategy (with the help of the following sections). This information can help discern whether a small company will be able to grow into a larger one. Many start-up firms fail to grow into their potential, either finding and maintaining a plateau or ultimately failing.

Study the competition

One way of deciding on a fintech firm's ability to scale is to study its potential competitors. (You can find those competitors by looking through accelerators and fintech award lists, or the firm may find itself in direct competition for sales on a regular basis.) How did those companies grow, and what can the company in question learn from that?

Understanding the competition can also help you assess the market saturation. What is the size of the market, and how well is it already being served? Does the complexity of the product enable multiple products to compete and win in that space? What is the company's unique selling proposition (USP)?

Listen to customers

Many investors will request a call with some of the fintech firm's customers to understand how they use the product and whether that usage is consistent with the firm's objectives. Recurring revenue is a major factor in determining a firm's viability and valuation. Therefore, it can be helpful to understand how important and "sticky" the product is to the client.

The ability to penetrate the market and increase sales is a vital factor in growing the business as well. Understanding how the product is distributed and delivered, as well as understanding what the client anticipates in customer service and future product development, is vital.

Ask about technology

Given all the recent technological advances, it can be difficult for investors to fully understand a company's technology stack. Does it do what the fintech firm claims it does? How scalable will the architecture and infrastructure be if the business grows quickly?

TIP

Some investors will use technical domain experts to ask the fintech firm the right questions to determine the technology's uniqueness or viability. Meanwhile, some independent firms have begun to produce objective, standardized scorecards on fintech firms that they sell to investors.

Inspire innovation

A founder may start their own fintech firm out of an ambition to build a more efficient and innovative product than currently exists. This ambition needs to be infectious, not only in selling the founder's vision to an investor but also to attract talented employees who want to join the journey of growing the business.

To scale, firms need to convey a passion that others will follow. This inspiration and passion is important to today's millennial workforce, where companies are likely to find the relevant new-technology skill sets. This is why some investors find the team (and their capability and credibility) important in determining which firms have growth capability.

No matter how "new" or "innovative" any technology or offering (fintech or otherwise), always pay attention to the "fundamentals" of the company. This means focusing on the company's sales and net profits and a solid balance sheet (where assets are comfortably greater than liabilities). And if the company is profitable year after year, that's the hallmark of a strong investment.

Too often, investors flock to a new company due to its alluring technology but the company may not have strong fundamentals (for example, maybe it's not profitable). If it isn't profitable (and especially if it has too much debt), this isn't an investment; it's a speculation. This means that the company hasn't proven itself yet (with profits) and it could be a failing investment if losses persist. Again, keep an eye on the numbers!

6

The Nickel Tour of Cannabis Investing

Whenever you're getting started on a new topic or trying to develop a new skill, you can benefit from having a general understanding of what's involved. It's sort of like reading the plot or synopsis of a movie or book before starting to watch or read it — or seeing the finished product before you start following the instructions to assemble it. You get the gist of what you're about to encounter, which serves as both a framework on which you can hang the details, and the context for more quickly and easily understanding those details.

The purpose of this chapter is to bring you quickly up to speed on the topic of investing in cannabis.

The Pros and Cons of Investing in Cannabis

The following sections present some of the most important pros and cons you should consider about investing in cannabis and leave the decision up to you.

Pros

TIP

The biggest motive people have for investing their money in any venture is profit. Chances are, you're curious about investing in cannabis because you want to profit from it, too. The industry is growing in leaps and bounds, and you want in on the action. Nothing wrong with that, but consider other benefits. Here's a complete list (or as complete as we can think of at the moment):

- **Profit:** As we already mentioned, this one is the biggie.
- **Getting in at or near the bottom of a new and exciting industry:** By investing in cannabis, you become a participant, not merely an observer, in the green rush, which can be thrilling.

- **Being able to tell people you know that your investment portfolio or retirement account includes cannabis stock:** This may sound silly, but being invested in cannabis says something about who you are and may help you engage in conversations you would otherwise be excluded from.
- **If you consume marijuana, getting to invest in a product you enjoy:** Investing in something you enjoy is one thing, but helping to make it more available to others feels even better.
- **If you invest in medical marijuana, investing in medical research and helping to bring those new medicines to market:** Your investment may potentially alleviate some of the world's physical and perhaps even mental suffering.

Life offers few choices to invest in a new industry in its infancy. You can think of investing in cannabis as what it would have been like to invest in alcohol three to five years before prohibition was repealed. How often do you get to participate in an industry at the dawn of legalization? Cannabis is a new industry. It presents an opportunity for an investor to be a pioneer.

Cons

Here's a list of reasons not to invest in cannabis that you should seriously consider before investing in this industry:

- Cannabis attracts money, and money attracts thieves. In addition, many novices eager to invest in cannabis are easy marks because they're eager and naïve and they have money — just the combination of traits a con artist is looking for.
- Many of the successful entrepreneurs in cannabis got their start in the black market, which attracts a very particular personality type. Leopards don't change their spots. Some savvy former black marketers have simply chosen a different crime — instead of dealing in illegal marijuana, they're now on the prowl for unsuspecting investors they can fleece.
- With lots of money flowing into the industry from eager investors, even legitimate cannabis stocks are overvalued. The more overvalued a stock is, the further the potential fall. Short sellers often target overvalued stocks just for this reason; then, when the stock price drops, they cash in and everyone else loses.
- Cannabis businesses struggle to be profitable due to numerous factors, including the high costs of complying with federal, state, and local marijuana laws;

increased security costs; increased bank fees; and the cost of specialized software.

- Cannabis stocks have an increased susceptibility to *dilution.* Companies issue and sell more shares to raise money, but that dilutes the value of existing shares. Although dilution is a risk for many kinds of stocks, it's especially problematic for a lot of marijuana stocks. Because of legal barriers that have prevented access to borrowing from banks, Canadian marijuana businesses have had limited choices available for generating capital to fund operations and growth. Many of these companies use an approach referred to as *bought deal financing,* whereby an investment bank or syndicate agrees to buy all of the securities a company issues at a predetermined price. This approach allowed marijuana companies to raise much-needed cash, but it also dramatically increased their numbers of outstanding shares and diluted the value of existing shares.
- Companies that grow cannabis are at risk of cannabis becoming a commodity, and if (when) that happens, prices and profits drop. *Commoditization* is the process by which a product becomes indistinguishable from other similar products, at which point the only factor distinguishing one product from another in the same market is price. All agricultural crops are commodities, and marijuana is an agricultural crop that may eventually be commoditized.

- Laws, and enforcement of those laws, are susceptible to change, and if they change in a direction that hurts cannabis businesses, their investors suffer as well.
- Supply-and-demand imbalances are common in the cannabis industry. These imbalances not only disrupt the supply chain but also negatively impact profits by creating market gluts (which drive down prices) or shortages (which increase costs and reduce demand); either way, profits suffer.
- If authorities don't crack down on illegal production and sales, legal businesses have a tough time competing.

TIP

Don't rule out investing in cannabis just because of this long list of potential drawbacks. You can considerably reduce your exposure to risk by doing your homework and investing in well-run companies. Be sure to properly research businesses and their management teams, and keep up on what's happening in the industry.

Businesses That Touch the Plant and Those That Don't

One of the first decisions to make before investing in cannabis is whether to invest in businesses that have contact with the plant or those that don't (often referred to as *ancillary* companies):

- **Plant-touching:** These businesses come into contact with the plant at some point during the growth, manufacturing, distribution, or sale. They include grow operations, manufacturers of infused products (MIPs), shipping firms, dispensaries, and licensed delivery services. Plant-touching businesses stand to profit most from cannabis, and they're also at the greatest risk of suffering losses when the industry takes a hit.

  TIP: If you decide to invest in a plant-touching business, consider a *vertically integrated company,* which means the business does its own cultivation, manufacturing, distribution, and sales. Vertically integrated companies are less susceptible to supply chain disruptions because they control their entire supply chain.

- **Ancillary:** These businesses serve the plant-touching businesses in some way. Perhaps the best-known ancillary business is Scotts, which provides fertilizer, pesticides, and disease control products, primarily for lawn care but also for agricultural operations, including cannabis cultivation companies. Other ancillary companies include manufacturers and dealers of equipment for cultivation operations; legal and accounting services that specialize in cannabis; software companies that develop point-of-sale and supply-chain managements systems; security equipment and service providers; and real estate groups that buy, sell, and rent land and buildings for cannabis businesses.

While plant-touching businesses carry the most potential for profit and risk, ancillary companies still stand to profit from the industry — and they have less exposure to risk.

According to a study published by Deloitte in 2016, ancillary businesses are estimated to be 2.5 times the size of the cannabis industry itself, so ancillary businesses stand to profit handsomely from the success of the cannabis industry.

Your Cannabis Investment Options

You can profit from legal cannabis businesses in several ways, depending on how directly you want to be involved. The most direct approach is to start your own cannabis business. The least direct approach is to trade cannabis-related securities, such as stocks, bonds, or exchange-traded funds (ETFs).

The following sections present different ways to invest in the cannabis industry to make you aware of the wide variety of options.

Start your own business

One approach to investing in the cannabis industry is to start your own business — either a plant-touching or an ancillary business. Here are some of the more popular opportunities cannabis entrepreneurs pursue.

- **Cultivator:** Cultivators start and grow plants from seeds; harvest the plants; separate the useable portion of the plants and properly dispose of the green waste; dry, cure, and trim the harvested bud; arrange for third-party lab tests to ensure the safety and quality of the product; pack and ship product to manufacturers and dispensaries; and track and report all processes as required by law to government regulatory agencies. Note that cultivation operations are the lowest profit-margin segment of the industry.

TIP: Cultivation is a great choice if you have a passion for the plant and a green thumb.

- **Manufacturer of infused products (MIP):** MIP is an industry term used to describe a company that makes marijuana-infused products, including concentrates such as wax and *shatter* (a glassy extract that can easily break), oils and tinctures, and lotions and edibles. This segment of the industry acts as a laboratory, as well as a processing plant. It may be even more tightly regulated than other segments of the industry, with additional rules and regulations that extend to manufacturing and commercial kitchens.

TIP MIP is a great choice for those who want to get more into the science of extracting active ingredients from the plant and using those extracts to create a wide variety of consumer products.

- **Processed product brand:** A processed product brand could be an MIP or a combined grow/MIP business that makes products and sells them to numerous retail outlets. For example, you could set up your own grow/MIP business to produce a line of infused chocolates that you sell to a variety of medical and recreational dispensaries. Another option is to create your own brand and develop unique products and then farm out the growing, manufacturing, and distribution operations to other businesses that specialize in those areas.
- **Retailer/dispensary owner:** Cannabis retailers run the dispensaries and other retail outlets that sell products directly to consumers. Depending on the rules and regulations in your area, you may be permitted to run a medical dispensary, an adult recreational dispensary, or a dispensary that serves both medical and adult recreational clients. This is like owning a liquor store but with more rules and regulations to follow.
- **Ancillary business:** Ancillary businesses you may want to consider include the following: nursery owner; man-

ufacturer or seller of grow lights; heating, ventilation, and air conditioning (HVAC) service provider specializing in ventilation and circulation for grow operations; packaging and labeling manufacturer/supplier; security service or manufacturer or supplier of security systems and equipment; marketing, public relations, or advertising specialist; real estate sales, rentals, or management (for more details, see the next section); legal, accounting, or consulting service provider; and banking and cash management services.

TIP

If you're interested in starting a business that comes in contact with the cannabis plant in any way, don't go it alone, and do be prepared for a high cost of doing business. Especially be sure to consult with a lawyer who has knowledge and expertise in helping businesses comply with state cannabis laws.

Invest in cannabis real estate

An often overlooked way to invest in cannabis is to buy land zoned for cannabis businesses or to buy land and have it zoned for such businesses and then sell or lease the land to cannabis businesses. You can even erect buildings on the land (or buy land with buildings suitable for certain types of businesses) and sell or lease the commercially improved land to businesses.

If you've seen the movie *The Founder,* about Ray Kroc, the founder of McDonald's, you probably remember his lawyer/advisor telling him, "You don't seem to realize what business you're in. You're not in the burger business; you're in the real estate business. You build an empire by owning the land." Kroc followed that advice and made a fortune buying the land on which McDonald's franchises were built and then leasing that land to the franchise owners.

TIP: You can take a similar approach to profit off the cannabis industry. However, you really need to know not only the cannabis industry and the real estate market, but also the rules and regulations in place that govern where (and what type of) cannabis businesses can be conducted on differently zoned plots of land.

If you're interested in investing in the cannabis real estate market, you have a couple of options:

- Sell or lease land or buildings to cannabis businesses. Be sure to lease the land/building at a premium that takes into account the limited real estate options for cannabis businesses.

  TIP: If this is the approach you decide to take, team up with a real estate broker and an attorney who understand the local cannabis market and the rules and regulations that are in place where you plan to invest. Profiting from cannabis-focused real estate investments requires specialized knowledge and expertise.

- Invest in a cannabis-focused real estate investment trust (REIT).

Buy and sell stocks

The most common way people invest in cannabis is to buy and sell stock in privately or publicly owned cannabis companies. Stocks provide you with a share of the company without your having to get your hands dirty or deal with the complex legal and regulatory issues (and other matters) of starting and running your own cannabis business. Of course, buying shares in an existing business leaves you with less control over the business, leaving the value of your shares in the hands of others. If they're innovative and intelligent and they manage the company effectively, your shares are likely to increase in value, but if they drop the ball, you're likely to lose money on your investment.

Investing in publicly traded companies has a couple of advantages:

- To list their stocks on public stock exchanges, companies must be a certain size and comply with stringent financial reporting standards, which provides a greater level of transparency for investors. In other words, you have more data on which you can base your investment decisions.

- Stock in publicly traded companies is a very liquid investment. You can convert your shares to cash almost immediately by listing them for sale on the exchange, assuming, of course, that someone's willing to buy the shares at a price you're willing to sell them for.

In this book, we assume you're investing in cannabis by buying and selling securities (stocks or bonds) in public or private companies and not by starting your own cannabis business or investing in real estate, which may be the focus of other books on investing in real estate. Be sure to get the information you need to research businesses and their management teams to determine whether they're likely to be profitable and good investments for you. You can then decide whether to invest in the company.

Diversify with ETFs and mutual funds

Most financial advisors recommend *diversification* as a way to reduce an investor's exposure to risk. A diversified investment portfolio contains both *stocks* (shares of ownership in a company) and *bonds* (like IOUs, short for "I owe you"); investments in numerous companies in a particular industry; and investments in various industries, such as cannabis, automobiles, pharmaceuticals, and energy.

One quick and easy way to diversify is to purchase shares of an ETF or mutual fund, both of which contain investments in a variety of businesses. The basic difference between the two is that shares of an ETF can be traded throughout the day like shares of stock, whereas shares of a mutual fund can be traded only after the markets close or before they open, because the share value is calculated a couple of hours after the markets close. You can find several cannabis-specific ETFs to invest in. Cannabis mutual funds are a rarer species.

The main drawback of cannabis ETFs and mutual funds is that a fund manager chooses the businesses to invest in, and fund managers may not be experts in the cannabis industry, so they may not make the best choices. You're generally better off doing your own research and making your own choices.

Consider private investment opportunities

Investing in private companies (in contrast to publicly traded companies) carries significantly more risk but has more potential for a higher return on investment (ROI). You basically have four options for investing in private companies depending on the business's stage of development:

- **Angel investing:** If you know someone who wants to start a cannabis business, you can bankroll the operation as an *angel investor,* usually in exchange for *ownership equity* (shares of stock) in the company or *convertible debt* (a loan that can later be converted to ownership equity). You can also join a group of angel investors, pooling your money to finance start-up businesses.

- **Venture capital investing:** One step up from angel investing is venture capital investing, which involves providing capital and expertise to take a promising start-up to the next level. As with angel investing, you can join venture capital groups to pool money and expertise.
- **Mezzanine investing:** One step up from venture capital investing is mezzanine investing, which involves private financing in the form of debt or preferred stock. (*Preferred stock* is a higher class of ownership than that provided by common stock. With preferred stock, you have first claim on any assets and earnings if the company struggles or folds.)
- **Private equity:** Private equity is financing that doesn't appear on public exchanges. It usually comes from funds and investors that invest directly in companies or that engage in buyouts of public companies, which results in those companies being delisted.

Private investing is usually the realm of high-net-worth individuals — and a perfect example of how the rich get richer.

How to Plan Your Investment Strategy

Prior to investing, give some thought to your investment strategy. Common investment strategies for any industry you choose to invest in include the following:

- **Value investing:** This strategy involves buying stocks in *undervalued companies* (companies that appear, based on their fundamentals, to be worth more than their share price indicates). Value investors believe that the markets are driven, to a large part, by emotion, and that by investing in profitable companies, they'll do better in the long run.

  What do we mean by fundamentals? *Fundamental analysis* is an approach to evaluating a security's intrinsic value based on a number of factors, such as the business's assets, liabilities, earnings, and management team; market conditions; the competitive environment; the overall state of the economy; legislation that is likely to impact the industry; analyst opinions; and so on. This method of stock analysis is commonly presented in contrast to *technical analysis* (an approach to predicting the future value of a security by analyzing trends in trading activity such as price movement and trading volume).

- **Growth investing:** This strategy involves investing in small companies you think have the potential to increase their earnings faster than their competitors or other companies in the industry. Unlike value investors, growth investors may be willing to pay more than book value for shares in the company. (*Book value* is the total amount a company would be worth if it sold all its assets and paid back all its liabilities.)
- **Momentum investing:** This strategy involves following trends in the prices of securities to capitalize on a company as its share price is rising or to short-sell shares as the share price drops. (To sell short, you borrow a stock and sell it. When the price drops, you buy back the stock and return it to the lender. The difference between the sell price and the buy price is your profit.)
- **Income investing:** This strategy focuses on earning a steady income from investments. It usually involves buying shares in companies that pay dividends, and buying bonds, which pay out interest on a consistent basis. Income investing is generally safer than value, growth, and momentum investment strategies, but the potential return may be lower.
- **Investing in what you know:** Many investors buy shares in only the companies they know or the companies that provide the products and services they like, believing that those products and services will

likely become increasingly popular among consumers, thereby driving the company's success. For example, if you're an Amazon Prime member, you may think to yourself, "Wow, Amazon is great. This company really has the potential to make it big," and, based solely on your personal experience, you decide to invest in Amazon.

- **Dollar-cost averaging:** With dollar-cost averaging, you buy shares regularly (for example, the same day each month), whether the share price is high or low, so you're not overpaying for a large quantity of shares at any one time. Of course, with this strategy, you're not getting a large quantity of shares at a low price, either.
- **Diversification:** This strategy involves spreading your investment dollars across a number of industries or a number of companies in the same industry to reduce your exposure to risk if one particular industry or company you invest in goes south.

In the context of cannabis investing, other strategies may include the following:

- Investing in ancillary businesses that serve the cannabis industry but don't touch the plant. Regardless of which cannabis businesses win or lose, ancillary businesses increase their earnings as the industry as a whole grows.

- Investing only in vertically integrated companies, which control their entire supply line. These companies also tend to be larger than those that are not vertically integrated.
- Investing exclusively in medical cannabis or exclusively in adult recreational cannabis, or investing a specific percentage in each.
- Investing in strong brands that have a presence in multiple states and perhaps even multiple countries.
- Investing in foreign markets such as the European Union.

7

Some Talk about NFTs

It all starts with *Bitcoin:* the original blockchain-based cryptoasset (covered in Chapter 4). With every run-up in Bitcoin prices, the Internet buzzes about crypto again. In fact, interest in non-fungible tokens (NFTs) has naturally surged with the Bitcoin tide.

With wild and exciting accounts of art-burning ceremonies and million-dollar NFTs, a mix of amazement, confusion, and even disdain surrounds this mostly "normal" but misunderstood digital creature.

In this chapter, we walk you through the basics of NFTs — what they are, how they work, and what they're used for.

What Is a Non-Fungible Good?

Although tokens themselves are a relatively new development, the idea of grouping fungible and non-fungible goods is not.

Think of dollar bills, shares of Microsoft stock, and Bitcoin — each represents a defined set where items within the set are *fungible*. Put simply, we don't care which dollar bills we receive as long as we receive the right quantity, because each dollar bill fulfills the same purpose and obligations as another.

Non-fungible goods are also a regular and far more prevalent part of our lives. Apples at the grocery store, orchids from the florist, and tickets to an upcoming concert — we inspect our fruit and our flowers to select the ones that are less bruised or wilted. With concerts, each ticket represents a different seat, and a front-row seat is not happily exchanged for a seat in the back of the theatre.

By their nature, non-fungible goods are more difficult to systematically record and track. For one, they require more information to be stored to denote their unique differences. We can't digitize the world, but there are many instances where we would greatly benefit from a reliable, transparent, and automated system designed to group, organize, and digitally track non-fungible things that are important to us. Here's where NFTs come into play!

An NFT is a unique digital identifier that's secured and stored on a public blockchain. One token is not interchangeable for another, and a token cannot be further divided.

What an NFT actually represents depends on the intent of the developers. Much like how a cryptocurrency — or a fungible token — can represent a global medium of exchange (Bitcoin), a utility token used to fuel smart contracts (Ether), or a financial security linked to shares in a fund, NFTs also differ in their current and potential uses.

Although general interest in NFTs has been minimal to nonexistent until recently, the development community has been teeming with fungible token activity for years. Following the successful launchings of Bitcoin (2009), Litecoin (2011), and Dogecoin (2013), a surge of projects followed, each spawning its own fungible tokens. Amidst this crypto-wave, developers began to envision a world of digital collectibles — the crypto-analogue of Beanie Babies (remember those?) and baseball cards. These projects required a different type of token standard to ensure the uniqueness and non-divisibility of each crypto-baby or crypto-card.

Finally, with the overwhelming success of CryptoKitties, a non-fungible token on Ethereum that debuted in 2017, the ERC-721 Non-Fungible Token Standard soon followed, serving as a blueprint for the development community. Since then, there's been an explosion of NFT projects, with tens of thousands of NFTs deployed on Ethereum alone at the time of writing.

Uses for NFTs

The NFT space is still in its infancy, but already the development community is teeming with ideas on how to put them to good use. The most natural use case — the one currently dominating the marketplace — is in tracking digital collectibles. From there, gaming items and digital media were natural extensions.

However, despite the recent explosion of NFTs, the current implementations are still rather limited in their scope, and mostly surround monetization of collectibles. The industry has also been hampered by the get-rich-quick mentality that has plagued crypto-space in general and has also attracted many unscrupulous players.

Still, many interesting use cases for NFTs are on the horizon. Some of these could truly disrupt the way people validate, track, and assign ownership of unique and esoteric items or work to effectively democratize content creation and distribution. Imagine taking the costly detective work out of verifying the ownership history of a rare collectible. Or imagine a world where expensive eBay auctions include proof of ownership on the Ethereum blockchain. Much attention is centered on speculation right now, but the potential value added by these exciting possibilities far overshadow the headlines announcing the latest NFT millionaires and NFT scam artists.

TIP The cryptocurrency world was also met with a similar breadth of reactions, ranging from deep skepticism to enthusiastic acceptance. But as governments and major financial institutions began to accept Bitcoin and Ether, the promise of the underlying technology came to the forefront of discussions. Although NFTs have the benefit of following their crypto-frontrunners (who themselves are still quite young), we need much more time to see how the NFT ecosystem will evolve and what it will spawn next.

How an NFT Works

TIP People often confuse the NFT itself with what the NFT was built to represent. An *NFT* is a cryptographically secure digital record that verifies your ownership of or access to, say, a piece of digital art — sort of like how your car title verifies ownership of your vehicle. You don't really own the car in your possession without the title, and you don't really own the CryptoKitty in your collection of JPEGs without the corresponding NFT.

For example, consider the cryptocollectible known as Mutant Ape Yacht Club (MAYC). This strange new collection of mutant apes (who may or may not be part of a yacht club?) is the latest rage among NFT collectors. But what exactly does it mean to own a particular MAYC?

When browsing MAYCs for sale on OpenSea (one of the NFT marketplaces), you notice provocative graphics and characteristics presented on the marketplace platform. What you're seeing are the visual representations of each individual MAYC — but the NFT itself is the unique digital code that's secured on the Ethereum blockchain.

For instance, consider MAYC #7632. Purchasing this NFT means that you're now the rightful owner of record of TokenID 7632, which is in storage in the contract account `0x60e4d786628fea6478f785a6d7e704777c86a7c6` on the Ethereum blockchain. All transfers of ownership will be memorialized on the blockchain so that provenance of MAYC #7632 and its current rightful owner can always be known.

TIP

As of this writing, 17,993 MAYCs exist across 11,859 holders. You can check out the individual details and ownership of each unique MAYC at `https://etherscan.io/token/0x60e4d786628fea6478f785a6d7e704777c86a7c6`.

The digital art you purchase is easy to duplicate. (Pressing the Print Screen key on the keyboard requires little to no training.) However, because the NFT is secured on a public blockchain, it's far more difficult to illegally transfer, duplicate, or otherwise hack. The beauty of NFTs lies in the underlying technology — a nexus of smart contracts and distributed network of validators — that allows you to reliably and automatically verify who truly owns each of the 17,993 mutant ape NFTs.

Thus, our mutant apes are part of a greater decentralized ecosystem where records are kept in a public and trustless manner, which means that we don't need a trusted central party, such as Scotiabank, to maintain a reliable and secure system to track our mutant apes for us. In their peculiar way, these mutant apes are bringing further awareness to the burgeoning landscape of decentralized finance (DeFi) and decentralized autonomous organizations (DAOs).

The majority of NFTs are minted as ERC-721 tokens on Ethereum. Thus, the provenance of each token is memorialized on the public Ethereum blockchain. Each subsequent transaction is validated and executed by a distributed network of miners — much like the system securing the Bitcoin blockchain.

Because an NFT is secured on a robust and tested blockchain (to date, the Ethereum blockchain has never been hacked), developers of nascent projects can piggyback off the existing system in place to secure ownership records and reward systems within the latest sub-economy under development.

We caution though, that, although the Ethereum blockchain itself has yet to be hacked, individual smart contracts deployed on Ethereum have. Thus, the recommended practice is to use vetted libraries that provide prebuilt smart contracts implementing development standards that have been reviewed and finalized by the greater community of core developers.

How to Buy NFTs

If you're curious how to buy an NFT, you should know that it's quite easy. There are now many marketplaces where you can purchase NFTs, and OpenSea is just one of many venues. Later in this chapter, we walk you through how to set up a wallet to hold your NFTs and how to purchase your first NFT.

Before you jump ahead, though, we have two main considerations that we'd like to highlight.

Why buy NFTs?

First, should you buy NFTs? Maybe. It depends on your motivations.

If you plan to actually *use* the NFT, then yes — you should buy it! For instance, perhaps the NFT provides you entry to a venue or gives you the legal right to post certain digital media on your website. In these cases, your only legitimate course of action would be to purchase the NFT.

We also advocate checking out NFT marketplaces for educational or even entertainment purposes. Perhaps you simply want to know how to go through the motions of buying an NFT. Or, perhaps you're more likely to learn the underlying technology and explore additional use cases if you begin by purchasing an NFT.

TIP In any of these circumstances, the biggest question is, "Are you spending money that you would seriously regret losing?" If so, then you certainly should not buy NFTs.

NFTs as investments

TIP We think of investments from the lens of traditional investment management principles. The gist is that you should be well diversified and rebalance over time so that you bear less risk as you approach retirement.

We don't advocate individual stock-picking as a sound investment practice, nor do we advocate NFT-picking as an investment practice. But, as we mention earlier, we aren't opposed to setting aside money that you won't miss, in order to have a little fun. This fun might mean a trip to Mexico, a dinner at a swanky French restaurant, or mutant ape NFTs.

Of course, as the NFT asset class matures, you develop a better sense of the risk-return trade-off of various NFTs and their appropriate allocations, if any, within a well-diversified investment portfolio. After all, with Bitcoin now approaching a US$1 trillion dollar market cap, we all should consider allocating a (tiny) portion of any truly broadly diversified portfolio to Bitcoin. Of course, this is a far cry from putting relatively large amounts of money in individual "investments" — whether it's individual stocks or NFTs or baseball cards — in the hopes of hitting the jackpot.

The Impact of NFTs

Since the inception of blockchain in 2009, it has been disrupting numerous industries. However, the general concept of blockchain technology, especially in the mind of the mass consumer, was still beyond most people's comprehension. (The Internet, in its early days, also seemed like an unfathomable mystery to most people.)

Democratizing blockchain

NFTs democratized blockchain, making it accessible and extremely valuable to a wide variety of people. NFTs took a once costly and time-consuming activity — selling a collector's item — and made it instantaneous and verifiable, similarly to how email was a paradigm shift for sending a letter, which could take days or weeks to arrive at its destination. With email, you could instantaneously receive or send a written message anywhere in the world. NFTs are the same for ownership of unique digital items and, maybe someday in the future, they can represent tangible assets.

Blockchain is the underlying technology that powers NFTs. (You've probably heard about blockchain in passing, but you might not be aware of many of its aspects.) Blockchain is a *distributed ledger* system where information can securely and reliably be stored and where any modification of this stored information is governed by strict rules. For example, no single party can change data without the whole system being made aware of it. (You might not think that's an interesting strategy, but data before blockchain was secured by an admin who had godlike powers over the records.)

TIP

NFTs derive their value from being trustworthy records of provenance. You can record transactions between yourself and another party efficiently and verifiably on the system's blockchain. The record of the transfer of your NFT becomes an immutable shared memory, distributed across the world with strict built-in accountability features.

Representing ownership

NFTs can represent ownership of all sorts of items, including digital artworks and in-game elements, not just digital cats. These NFTs are typically purchased for Ethereum or Bitcoin on a *centralized exchange* (a platform that facilitates the transaction).

Trading between users

NFTs can be traded on a peer-to-peer basis without the need for an intermediary. In this model, the trade takes place directly between two people or groups instead of using one person (or company) as an intermediary for all trades to facilitate and monitor them. This means there's no need to rely on another party, like eBay or Amazon, to buy something from someone else; you can do it yourself using just your phone.

The internal exchange mechanisms that allow users to trade between themselves without an intermediary are called *decentralized exchanges* (DEXes), which enable you to sell your assets independently of a third party — they're becoming popular because centralized exchanges are vulnerable to theft. Exchanges run by a company require the system to be controlled by a single party, negating the power of blockchain and turning it against the user. If an item is stolen from a company exchange, it's nearly impossible to retrieve it again.

Enabling smart contracts

NFTs enable decentralized exchanges via *smart contracts* (computer scripts that run on those ledger nodes with access to data about the NFT). For example, when you purchase a CryptoKitty, you purchase a piece of unique digital art that has been coded with ownership that automatically changes when payment is made — all without the need for a third-party agent. This system reduces risk while expediting transactions by eliminating intermediaries. Similar to the email example we mention earlier, exchanging ownership instantaneously with anyone in the world is now possible.

Creating digital scarcity

The *CryptoKitties* team addressed the concept of digital scarcity for singular items by way of their digital collectibles. No two CryptoKitties are alike — each one is unique. Digital goods, which aren't a new concept, have seen real-world valuation. For example, *World of Warcraft*'s gold farmers use the Steam platform's online marketplace, where users can buy and sell in-game items across their PC's video game collection. However, this niche, which was limited to video games, lacked the features that blockchain affords. You can find numerous examples of hacking or cheating or developers influencing the ecosystem.

Digital collectibles hold immense potential that started with digital cats but has since moved on to all types of collectibles and art.

Solving problems

Adding NFT to the mix has changed how people perceive digital collectibles, as evidenced by the intense interest shown in digital collectibles such as CryptoPunks and other NFTs. A digital art enthusiast paid a whopping US$69.3 million for the NFT named *EVERYDAYS: THE FIRST 5000 DAYS*. The *Genesis* CryptoKitty NFT, the rarest in existence, sold for 246.926 Ether.

The size, scope, and long-term pedigree of these NFTs alleviate fears associated with cryptocurrencies, as the following list makes clear:

- **The central issuing authority problem:** When digital collectibles are created and issued and the market identifies the rarest or the most popular collectibles, nothing stops the creator from simply creating more. When this happens, it diminishes the value of the original collectibles, potentially making them worthless.
- **The provider dependency problem:** The existence of a digital collectible is dependent on the presence of the issuing authority. If a digital collectible is created and the initial creator ceases to exist, your digital collectibles also cease to exist. NFTs, on the other hand, live on distributed ledgers that replicate. If the token economics

of the blockchain are in line with the network's nodes, your NFT is safe. Most NFTs just contain the smart contract, which in many cases points to a URL (huge risk, since the host could be shut down or the content could be changed on their end). The image might be too large or it might simply be too tedious to integrate.

- **Purpose and function of digital collectibles:** Physical collectibles are popular because of their intended purpose. If you collect art, for example, it can be worth a lot of money, and it serves a purpose by hanging on your wall as an item of beauty and status.

TIP

With the help of blockchain technologies, these problems have been solved, which has made people far more willing to invest in digital collectibles outside the niche of video games. If NFT digital collectibles hold their value the same way a physical collectible does, an entirely new world of collecting will come to life.

What's in Your Wallet? How to Set Up MetaMask

MetaMask is a free browser extension and smartphone app that allows you to interact with the Ethereum (ETH) blockchain. It lets you log in to dApp websites with your wallet keys and send and receive coins from your cryptocurrency wallet. (The term *dApp* stands for decentralized application.)

MetaMask is a *hot wallet*, a tool connected to the Internet that enables you to store, receive, and send ETH and other tokens. All web-based wallets are hot wallets and are the most insecure of all the cryptocurrency wallets. By contrast, a *cold wallet* (sometimes referred to as a *hardware wallet* or *offline wallet*) is not connected to the Internet. Given that MetaMask is a hot wallet, it isn't a secure way to store value.

TIP Use hot wallets only for small transactions that you execute right away.

As of this writing, MetaMask has suffered no major hacks. The MetaMask is a *hierarchical deterministic wallet* (HD wallet) that automatically generates a hierarchical treelike structure of private and public addresses to back up your wallet. You then don't have to manually generate those pairs for backups. MetaMask also has an active community of developers who regularly update its code base. The main risk you face in using MetaMask is from *phishing* attacks, where a scam artist sends you a fraudulent message to trick you into revealing your passwords and usernames.

TIP Phishing attacks are common, and your wallet's password and recovery phrase are the target. Never, under *any* circumstances, give anyone access to your password or passphrase. You can prevent phishing attacks by religiously avoiding opening these items:

- Pop-up ads
- Suspicious emails
- Links in suspicious ads or emails

MetaMask also allows you to manage your identity online. When a dApp wants to run a transaction and write to the Ethereum blockchain, MetaMask acts as a secure interface for you.

TIP That said, the MetaMask wallet's security is insufficient to keep large sums. Keep the amount stored here equivalent to what you would be willing to have in your own wallet or purse. If you need to store more tokens, consider using a hardware wallet, like a Trezor or Ledger hardware wallet. Also, buy the hardware wallet directly from the manufacturer. In some recent Amazon scams, the devices were compromised before being sent to the buyer.

To set up a MetaMask wallet, follow these steps:

1. **Navigate to the MetaMask website at** `https://metamask.io`.

   You can see the support that MetaMask gives you. It works on the Brave, Chrome, Edge, and Firefox browsers. At the time of writing, it doesn't support Safari, but it does offer an iPhone app, as well as an Android app. We're using Chrome for this example.

2. **Click the Download Now button and then click Install MetaMask for Chrome.**
3. **At the Chrome web store, click Add to Chrome.**

   When your browser is done downloading MetaMask, you see the option to either import an existing wallet or set up a new MetaMask wallet.

4. **Click the Add a New Wallet link.**

   MetaMask asks you to send some data to them. It won't reveal your identity, but it's used to make the service better. You can opt out if you want to.

5. **Create a password.**

   This is a password just for MetaMask. It isn't the recovery phrase or the private keys for your wallet. The password is secondary security.

> You're taken to the security-phrase screen, where you're prompted to write down a recovery phrase. Do *not* skip this section.

6. **Write down the words clearly, and store the paper in a safe place.**

TIP: You may want to go so far as laminating the piece of paper and storing it in a vault. You need the recovery phrase if you lose your password or device.

7. **On the next screen, confirm the recovery phrase so that MetaMask knows that you wrote it down properly.**

   After you've correctly entered the recovery phrase, you can get into your MetaMask wallet.

   TIP: The MetaMask team is always making updates. Check back frequently to see what they've added.

8. **Within your wallet, navigate to Settings and select the General tab to change your currency conversion and choose the primary currency.**

   This is how all the holdings in your MetaMask wallet are valued.

9. **Choose a language.**

   If you navigate to the Advanced section, you can reset the account and clear your entire transaction history. You can also find some other controls, including advanced gas controls.

10. **Navigate to the main page and click the three dots on the right side of your wallet.**

    There you can see your account details, including your Ethereum address. You need your Ethereum address to receive Ethereum-based tokens. This is as simple as scanning the QR code with your smartphone. If you already have a crypto-exchange app, you can skip the next section, "How to Set Up Coinbase."

TIP

A *cryptocurrency wallet,* like MetaMask and others, allows you to store cryptocurrency, like ETH. You need to use an *exchange platform,* like Coinbase, to convert dollars (or any real-world currency) to cryptocurrency that you then store in your wallet. Exchange services often provide a wallet, but you can use any wallet with any exchange. The Coinbase Wallet, for instance, is a separate app available to use with a Coinbase account. However, you don't have to have a Coinbase account to use the Coinbase wallet, and vice versa.

How to Set Up Coinbase

Coinbase (`www.coinbase.com`) is a popular exchange service that allows you to connect your bank account to a cryptowallet and purchase from an ever-growing list of assets.

TIP

You must be at least 18 years old and have a government-issued photo ID to set up Coinbase. Passport cards are not accepted. You also need a computer or smartphone connected to the Internet. Coinbase verifies your phone number via text messages.

Create your Coinbase account

Coinbase charges no fee to create or maintain your account, but it does charge transaction fees. Follow these steps to create your Coinbase account:

1. **Go to** `www.coinbase.com` **from a browser on your computer, or download and open the Coinbase app on an Android or iOS phone.**
2. **Click or tap Get Started.**
3. **Enter your legal name, your email address, and a password.**

   TIP: Make sure to write down your password and the seed phrase that's generated for you, and store both in a secure place. (The *seed phrase* is a random set of words that are used to recover your wallet. Think of them as a special password.)
4. **Provide your place of residence.**
5. **Select the check box and click Create Account from a computer, or tap Sign Up from a mobile phone.**

   Coinbase sends a verification email to your email address.

6. **Navigate to the email and select Verify Email Address to verify your Coinbase account.**

   TIP: Make sure the email came from `no-reply@coinbase.com`.

   You're taken back to Coinbase.

7. **Sign in using the email and password you created initially to complete the email verification process.**

Verify your phone number

After you've created a Coinbase account and verified your email address, you need to verify your phone number, too. Just follow these steps:

1. **Sign in to Coinbase.**
2. **When prompted, select your country and add your mobile phone number.**
3. **Click the Send Code pop-up from a computer or tap Continue on your mobile phone.**
4. **Enter the code that Coinbase texts to your phone number and then click Submit (from your computer) or Continue (from your phone).**

Add your personal information

You add the information shown on your valid government-issued photo ID, so have it handy when you complete these steps:

1. **Stay in the Coinbase app.**

   After verifying your phone number, Coinbase asks you to submit a photo of your ID.

2. **Enter your first name, last name, date of birth, and address, and answer a list of questions, including the following:**

   What do you use Coinbase for?

   What is your source of funds?

   What is your current occupation?

   Who is your employer?

3. **Click Continue to finish the process.**

This step completes the application process. You need to wait until you receive further instructions via email to know that your account is approved. At that point, you can complete the next section.

Verify your identity and add your bank account

When you receive the additional instructions mentioned in the previous section, do the following:

1. **Sign in to your Coinbase account.**
2. **Complete the ID verification process.**

TIP: Set up two-factor verification, such as a time-based one-time password (TOTP), to help protect against unauthorized account access. Google offers one called Authenticator, which you can find on the Apple App Store or the Google Play Store.

Add funds to your wallet

If you haven't already done so, send some ETH to your MetaMask wallet. Just sign in to your wallet and follow these steps:

1. **On the main page of your wallet, click the Buy button.**

   From there, you have the choice to add tokens via a wallet you already have or via Wyre.

2. **Select Directly Deposit Ether and copy your MetaMask wallet address.**

3. **Navigate back to your Coinbase wallet and use it to send yourself enough ETH to buy a CryptoKitty and cover the fees for the exchange.**

   The price of processing your purchase changes daily — review the fee before processing the transaction.

4. **With funds in your MetaMask wallet, you can navigate back to the CryptoKitties website at** `www.cryptokitties.co` **to purchase your first kitty (a common example of a first NFT purchase).**

If you need additional help setting up a wallet or an exchange app, check out *Blockchain For Dummies*, 2nd Edition, by Tiana Laurence, or *Ethereum For Dummies*, by Michael G. Solomon (both published Wiley). These books cover this topic in greater detail.

8

ESG Strategies and Investment Decisions

Typical equity-based investment funds are either *actively managed* (the portfolio manager decides where and what to invest in) or *passively managed* (a fund tends to follow market indexes, with no active decisions made by the portfolio manager). This approach applies equally to environmental, social, and governance (ESG) funds:

- Some managers determine their ESG universe based on a given number of stocks, which naturally increases the *active risk* (the measure of risk in a portfolio that is due to active management decisions) within a portfolio.
- Other managers take a more passive approach by following a specified index and its composition of

securities, some of which may exclude given stocks (for example, fossil fuels, tobacco, and arms-related stocks). In other words, the index company selects the portfolio of companies that the fund manager then follows.

This chapter investigates how different equity-based strategies have been applied to the growing demand for ESG exposure. This includes how ESG factors are integrated into existing funds and strategies, including adjusting index-based or sector- and theme-based approaches. This chapter runs through the basics of getting started, discusses both active and passive investment approaches, and notes where the respective ESG scores and risks can be recognized within given strategies.

TIP

Awareness of the benefits of ESG integration is increasing, and the types of applications are growing. What do we mean by "ESG integration"? Glad you asked. *ESG integration* is the systematic and explicit inclusion of material ESG factors into investment research, analysis, and decision-making. This is one of three broad approaches to adding ESG analysis into investment decisions, along with screening and thematic investing. All three ESG procedures can and often are applied simultaneously.

Just the Basics: An Overview of the Process

Most investors will begin the process of ESG integration by following four common steps:

1. **Qualitative analysis:** Collecting relevant intelligence from different sources, including company reports and research, and determining material factors that are influencing the company. When we say *material factors,* we mean financially material issues that are most likely to impact the financial condition of a company and are consequently most important to investors.
2. **Quantitative analysis:** Measuring the effect of material financial factors on equities in existing portfolios or the wider universe, and modifying valuation models accordingly.
3. **Investment decisions:** Using this analysis to decide whether to buy (or increase weighting), hold (or maintain weighting), or sell (or decrease weighting).
4. **Active ownership/stewardship:** Using the prior analysis to inform company engagement and proxy voting decisions. This information can be used to support

any future monitoring and investment analysis and to advise subsequent investment decisions.

After this process, the evaluation of material issues from ESG factors can determine the following:

- Financial and financially material ESG factors
- The potential effect of material financial and ESG factors on company, sector, economic, and country performance
- Investment decisions to buy, hold, trim, or exit positions

TIP

Adopting such an approach may involve changes to an investor's processes, which requires a development of the skills needed to decide how ESG issues may impact individual company performance. Particularly, investors need to develop the skills to identify and integrate material ESG concerns, which are believed to affect company and investment performance. This can reduce the analysis required for those companies where ESG issues aren't considered to be material at that time. Investors who are collecting ESG information from multiple sources — including company reports, filings, and ESG research providers — to identify the most material ESG issues per company or sector build this skill and experience over time.

To achieve stock-level integration, investors will then commonly adjust financial statement forecasts and valuation discount rates in their financial models to reflect material ESG factors, as well as any industry-related ESG issues. Given that companies can be scored using material ESG characteristics, portfolios can be constructed to overweight or underweight individual securities that match such characteristics in an optimized tilt. This balances the potentially opposing features of increasing a portfolio's ESG score and decreasing the portfolio's tracking error relative to its benchmark, thus permitting investors to integrate the ESG influence. Therefore, ESG indicators have been added to traditional financial measures, taxes, and other fundamental information to assess the value of public companies.

However, many early-stage investors in ESG have primarily used simpler approaches, employing negative screening techniques, which effectively exclude certain types of stocks such as alcohol, tobacco, and fossil fuels. Alternatively, investors have expanded on this approach by focusing on given themes or sectors, either from an exclusion perspective, as per individual stocks, or from positive screening where they add stocks, sectors, or themes that exhibit positive ESG scores. This has been particularly true in Europe, where the largest quantity of ESG-related assets under

> management reside. This is largely because companies haven't traditionally reported or explicitly identified material ESG data that could affect their financial performance, so the only way to accomplish that is through investors proactively engaging with companies.

On a positive note, there are more industry-wide efforts to increase the standardization of ESG data and reporting requirements, which should greatly improve access to data. As standardization continues to improve, more institutional investors should follow the material ESG factor integration approach. This is already true for the United States, where ESG integration into analysis of listed equity investments is the most common ESG approach. However, greater integration in the United States isn't due to U.S. companies reporting material ESG factors any better than elsewhere, so greater standardization of ESG data providers' input is still required.

Active ESG Strategies

The development of ESG investing is being driven by bottom-up pressure from asset owners and top-down policy initiatives. More investors are now concentrating on maximizing ESG performance through risk-return constraints, rather than the more traditional approach of prioritizing risk-adjusted returns. In other words, more investors are now focused on maximizing ESG performance, subject to their own risk-return limits, rather than purely focusing on an investment's return subject to the degree of risk taken to achieve it (hedge funds and investors commonly refer to this as the *Sharpe ratio,* named for the economist who developed it).

Market participants suggest that active managers have traditionally focused on issues that are most relevant to underlying investment performance through fundamental bottom-up approaches, and so they have the aptitude to explore and evaluate ESG issues that are financially material. Moreover, active management approaches have focused on shareholder engagement with management in a consistent manner. Active managers, due to their deep knowledge of companies, should play an important role in engaging with management on material ESG data points, providing a value-added proposition that could positively sway company behavior and push sustainable long-term value for investors.

Because ESG issues are embedded with business issues, a single source of data isn't always sufficient to decide on investment pros and cons. Many active ESG strategies will have a team of fundamental equity and credit research analysts, supported by expertise from an in-house ESG team, who assess material ESG themselves instead of relying solely on external ESG data

> providers. These multiple sources of data should provide greater flexibility and the capacity to concentrate on the most material issues relevant to the investment theme. Active ownership should also entail communicating with firms to enhance their ESG policies and practices. Engagement beyond formal data can be more meaningful than the data on its own, as each of the data providers has a slightly different approach to evaluating ESG practices in companies.

Also, ESG analysis is equally essential to active fundamental analysis. Issues that are material to performance are constantly evolving, so investors' approach to corporate engagement and analysis should also continue to evolve. Where analysts are directly engaged in the business context, procedures, and industrial requirements of a company and its sector, they should also be on top of ESG issues that are evolving, which provides confidence in measuring and establishing the credibility of the fundamental investment process.

Furthermore, they should be able to attune allocations to reflect changes to ESG assessments as they arise. This ability to respond immediately to changing dynamics can allow active managers to unearth opportunities or risks that could be missed by passive ESG strategies, which may be more important in the current environment as corporations struggle to comply with changing disclosure regulations and investor expectations.

How to Analyze the Impact of Different ESG Scores

TIP

There's an increasing body of evidence that corporations prioritizing ESG issues generate superior long-term performance across a variety of metrics, including sales growth, return on equity (ROE), and even *alpha* (a measure of market outperformance). Companies pursuing a stakeholder approach to value creation by integrating ESG into their long-term strategies are able to attract the best talent, develop loyal customer bases, benefit from sound corporate governance oversight, moderate risk, and push profitable growth by investing in sustainable innovations. So, shareholders should still benefit, but not at the expense of employees, customers, suppliers, or the community.

Consequently, modeling a business around ESG factors can be an underappreciated source of sustainable competitive advantage, given the strong business fundamentals and ability to create market outperformance that such companies possess. Furthermore, this has been confirmed by testing the effect of material ESG scores on stock returns.

Material ESG scores, which identify and evaluate only those issues that are financially important to a company, enhance forecasts of financial performance in comparison to total ESG scores. This finding has been particularly true for total ESG scores (an aggregate of the individual scores given to the ESG issues) as opposed to ESG score changes (the relative change in a total ESG score), which is in line with the long-term value-generation attribute of ESG performance:

- **Total ESG scores** are claimed to be a more accurate forecaster of longer-term business performance.
- **ESG score changes** are guided by short-term events and accordingly have a greater influence on short-term performance.

This analysis can be used to validate the view that long-term material ESG factors are currently mispriced by the market. So, by having a more qualitative incorporation of material ESG data in the valuation approach, investors could benefit from this mispricing. As long as such information isn't transparently available, there is a competitive advantage for those analysts who can deliver such information, and given that the market has been slow to adapt, this mispricing may be available for some time.

Moreover, if this information is combined with data provided in a business sustainability assessment questionnaire, they're even more significant as a forecaster of financial returns than broadly available public information, particularly for companies in industry sectors that exhibit more environmental risks.

Watch Out: Risks and Disclosures

Investment managers need to be able to measure and understand risk in order to manage it. Risk management is the essence of investment management, so analyzing ESG risk factors, alongside more traditional statistical and quantitative risk factors, helps deepen understanding of potential downside risks. Correspondingly, time invested now in evolving investment research to integrate an ESG framework will help differentiate the funds that will be successful in the future.

In addition, analyzing more conventional quantitative-risk measures, such as tracking error or *beta* (the volatility of a security or portfolio in comparison to the market as a whole), alongside more qualitative ESG risk metrics ensures a multidimensional perspective.

TIP

As the quality and availability of ESG data and analysis continue to evolve, asset managers who understand the data can use it to further inform their investment evaluation. ESG data should provide new perspectives to unearth any risks that are hidden in the balance sheets and financial ratios and identify new investment opportunities. In addition, the information offered by proprietary ESG scoring and ranking techniques has helped investors build a granular picture of corporations' ESG performance. This has been driven by the increasing scope of mandatory ESG disclosure obligations.

For example, under the EU's Non-Financial Reporting Directive (introduced in January 2017 but currently being revised), listed EU companies with more than 500 employees need to disclose a range of information in their annual reports concerning employee, environmental, and social issues; respect for human rights; and corruption. Moreover, voluntary standards and frameworks, such as the Carbon Disclosure Project (CDP), the Financial Stability Board's Task Force on Climate-related Financial Disclosures (TCFD), and the Science-Based Targets (SBT) initiative, are encouraging more standardized reporting that should lead to more informed ESG scores.

TIP

Meanwhile, the Global Reporting Initiative (GRI; `www.globalreporting.org`), the most widely used reporting standard, allows companies to determine which issues are material for reporting purposes, ultimately allowing investors to compare companies' ESG performance and companies to incorporate guidelines into financial reporting. In addition, the Sustainability Accounting Standards Board (SASB; `www.sasb.org`) takes an investor's viewpoint to recognize which sustainability metrics are anticipated to have a material effect on the financial state or operating performance of companies. The definitions that SASB has determined as material per industry and sector have become reference points for many market participants.

How Companies with Higher ESG Scores Outperform

Investors have traditionally been concerned that sustainable investing requires a risk/return trade-off when investing in corporations with strong ESG practices, an approach that provides lower risk but also lower return. This may have become more of an issue in recent years as more ESG-focused investment vehicles have been offered to investors and a record number of assets have been invested in ESG funds. Nevertheless, analysis suggests that in recent years, and during the COVID-19 pandemic, ESG-based funds have performed well.

One explanation for this could be that companies with high ESG scores have already succeeded in achieving better governance, lowering operational risk, and building in greater flexibility due to better employee relations and more reliable supply chains and have, thus, minimized the risk to their business reputation. Consequently, they tend to be of higher quality, to exhibit lower volatility, and to be larger in market capitalization and more mature, with higher earnings and dividend yields. These factors have allowed them to protect their earnings better and, therefore, to have gained wider acceptance than companies with lower ESG metrics.

Conversely, a counter-explanation is that ESG funds' outperformance can be better explained by what they *don't* hold than what they do. Actively managed ESG funds have strict selection criteria, actively engage with companies in their portfolios, and avoid poorly rated ESG companies and sectors. Such funds are often underweight in, or exclude entirely, sectors such as airlines, tobacco manufacturers, and energy sourced from coal, oil, and gas, thus avoiding underperformance of those stocks in their overall return.

Put more succinctly, generally speaking, buying "best-in-class" stocks and selling the "worst in class" should have generated an annualized excess return in recent years. Historically, this could have been explained away by cyclical rotation in and out of given sectors in line with the cyclical performance of macro indicators. However, a paradigm shift seems to have been observed in recent years, initially driven by climate change concerns but exacerbated more recently by the impact of the pandemic.

TIP

Further examination of the return drivers for different components within ESG shows that environmental components exhibit positive excess return by the outperformance of "best-in-class" stocks and underperformance of "worst-in-class" stocks. Alternatively, social and governance components appear to generate their positive excess return from the poor performance of "worst-in-class" stocks. Moreover, the social component seems to have come to the fore in more recent years and is likely to receive even more attention after the pandemic.

TIP

To compute ESG ratings requires a mixture of qualitative, quantitative, and engagement-based approaches by identifying material ESG risks and opportunities for each sector, allocating weights to the key indicators based on their materiality, and then combining quantitative ESG ratings with analysts' financial recommendations.

Take It Easy: Passive Strategies

Two prominent investment developments in recent years have been the increase in assets that are passively managed and the growth in sustainable investing. Replicating both these developments, index-based funds that feature ESG factors have grown in both number and assets. The majority of sustainably invested assets remain in actively managed ESG funds, but net flows into passively managed ESG funds have outstripped net flows into active funds for four of the past five years. Investors have been drawn to passive strategies, such as passive index funds and exchange-traded funds (ETFs), in general due to their performance since the financial crisis in 2009 and the demand for lower-cost exposure to market beta.

Meanwhile the shift to ESG indexes has seen responsible investing command an increasing share of the global ETF market, and this trend is likely to increase further. Index benchmarks are now being used by fund managers as tools to position investor selections and to redirect investment flows.

The following sections go over the pros and cons of passive methods for integrating ESG into investment decisions.

The pros

Although many ESG investors use an active stock selection approach, passive (index-based) methods can also be well suited for ESG-driven portfolios. An index's selection criteria for ESG issues can range across many different approaches, including ESG quality, sustainability, and thematic and sector exclusions. Passive strategies have democratized access to the financial markets at a low cost, characteristics that are consistent with an emphasis on passive ESG goals, and both approaches are data driven.

Assuming that an appropriate index, either ESG or non-ESG, has been selected, asset managers can create one of the following routes to offering, for example, a passively managed ESG fund:

- **Purchase an ESG index license,** which provides the initial investment universe of constituent companies, and design a fund to replicate the index.
- **Purchase an ESG index license and apply ESG methodology approaches,** such as exclusionary screens, ESG integration and/or thematic filters, to refine company selection and narrow the investment universe to a smaller set of companies based on defined rules.
- **Weight the index constituents once they're selected.** They can do this following index rules, such as by market capitalization, equal weighting, or "tilting" to underweight or overweight given companies based on specific rules.

TIP

Given that passive investment funds are based on indexes, they share certain features that are appealing to investors who want to use their investments to contribute toward positive ESG impacts:

- They provide simplicity, because the indexes they're based on are transparent and rules-based and are, therefore, easy to understand.
- Because the underlying portfolio seeks to replicate the index, the companies in the portfolio will change as the constituents of the index are revised.
- They create performance benchmarks and help evaluate the broad performance of ESG and non-ESG universes. This generally requires less maintenance than for actively managed funds, so they tend to have lower fees and operating expenses.
- However, investors should note that the "low-cost" character of passive investing via ETFs and index funds is significantly different in the ESG framework.

Net total expense ratios for passive funds and ETFs are generally higher than in the non-ESG universe, with passive ESG products levying a wide range of fees, and the median expense ratio of equity ETFs being in the range of 40 to 50 basis points. Investment firms justify this additional expense through the need to perform additional due diligence or screening for ESG funds, but in practice they generally depend on ESG vendor ratings and third-party data. Nonetheless, market acceptance of higher expense ratios reveals an acknowledgment of the due diligence requirements for ESG analysis.

Passive managers tracking broad-based indexes can use ESG integration to overweight companies with better ESG scores and underweight peer companies. Furthermore, some passive managers deliberately differ from conventional benchmarks' industry weights by excluding controversial companies, such as fossil fuel companies.

The cons

Critics of passively managed funds feel that ESG variations of those funds are just compounding the fact that conventional indexes, such as the S&P 500, don't reflect the true economy, reward size, and liquidity, and take no account of, for example, corporate governance. Therefore, any funds with traits inherited from such indexes are inconsistent with the aim of moving toward genuine sustainability.

Also, passive strategies are normally applied by utilizing a single third-party source for ESG research and data that rely heavily on voluntary company disclosure. This can create limitations in the quality, disclosure, and other biases inherent with ESG data, as this data is backward-looking, meaning that investors are missing a complete risk-reward analysis, which may result in skewed allocations to portfolio optimization and sector weighting.

In addition, different third-party ESG rating providers often have contradictory views on the same company, which is difficult for the passive manager to understand as they're unaware of the source of the analysis, criteria, or assumptions made in giving a company a certain score in the first place.

This is further exacerbated by the number of holdings in the chosen passive index, leading to a lack of in-depth understanding of the companies' fundamentals and how the fund will be able to pursue active ownership strategies, such as ensuring company engagement, filing shareholder resolutions, and developing proxy voting guidelines to ensure improvements in a company's ESG policies and practices. Many observers are calling for greater commitment to improving corporate ESG practices from passive managers entering the sustainable investing space. Particularly with respect to proxy voting records, the largest index fund managers — BlackRock, Vanguard, and State Street, which together hold around 80 percent of indexed assets — have been criticized in the past for regularly voting in support of management and in opposition to ESG shareholder resolutions. Given the size of their holdings, their support is often vital in securing such shareholder resolutions.

On the contrary, concerns aimed at indexlike characteristics are less relevant to passive funds based on narrower thematic or industry-focused indexes, such as clean energy, where filters ensure that all companies in a fund contribute to the specific theme. Further examples of ESG issues addressed by sustainable investors include environmental issues, such as clean technology, water use and conservation, sustainable natural resources, and agriculture, while social issues include human rights, gender and racial equity, and workplace concerns. Also, instead of focusing on a way to determine ESG risks, a new generation of ESG benchmarks is being established to have a measurable impact, such as helping to meet climate transition goals under the Paris Agreement.

Finally, while active managers are more concentrated on stock-picking portfolios, many institutional investors prefer to employ ESG investing through optimized benchmarking portfolios that fit their strategic asset allocation (SAA) policy. For example, they typically define an SAA portfolio based on market-capitalization indexes and observe their investments by computing any tracking error between the invested portfolio and the strategic portfolio. Therefore, they accept a maximum level of tracking error, prompting some managers to build ESG-based, optimized portfolios by minimizing the tracking error with respect to the cap-weighted index for a given ESG excess score.

Effectively, this indexation with an ESG overlay approach offers investors a competitive solution to compete on price with traditional market-cap passive strategies. Consequently, ESG index tracker funds can offer a feasible, cost-effective solution for passive investors, who, while mandatory holders of the index, are seeking a pragmatic solution to escape the unsustainable practices of many listed companies.

Relative Returns and Performance of ESG Stocks

The general mantra from researchers and the market, based on more recent performance metrics, suggests that ESG investors don't have to compromise on performance in order to pursue competitive market returns. Positive screening strategies based on ESG scores (whether created externally by ESG scoring providers or in-house by dedicated analysts) can raise the ESG quality of both passive and active traditional and smart beta portfolios, without reducing risk-adjusted returns. However, instead of focusing on maximizing financial performance from ESG criteria, many investors are now concentrating on maximizing ESG performance subject to risk-return constraints.

Most market participants have reviewed the performance of ESG portfolios before and after the stock market sell-off caused by fears over the COVID-19 pandemic in 2020. During this period, the S&P 500 ESG Index, which tracks large U.S. companies with high ESG ratings, outperformed the established S&P index by 0.6 percent. Similarly, the MSCI Emerging

Markets ESG Leaders Index, and the more Asia-focused MSCI AC Asia ESG Leaders Index, outperformed their parent indexes by 0.5 percent and 3.83 percent, respectively. Indeed, BlackRock calculated that 88 percent of a globally representative selection of sustainable indexes outperformed their non-sustainable peers over the same period. And this isn't a new phenomenon — BlackRock has also suggested that similar outperformance was seen during market downturns from 2015 to 2016 and also in 2018.

Of course, some investors may see the demand for ESG stocks with high ratings as a potential bubble, given the weight of funds that are deployed in those stocks. Could the current outperformance lead to overstretched valuations, which in turn may lead to long-term underperformance? This is causing some investors to analyze stocks where their current ESG ratings aren't so high, but they're making credible efforts to improve their ratings through strong, sustainable business practices.

The other regular explanation for ESG outperformance is that, through their exclusion or reduced weighting policies due to fossil fuel screens, most ESG funds have low exposure to fossil fuel assets, which has protected their portfolios when oil prices and energy stocks have fallen. Some analysts suggest that such factors account for only a small amount of any outperformance and propose that, apart from the momentum of investors' buying supporting prices, better supply chain management and corporate governance have contributed to their effectiveness.

To maintain high ESG ratings, corporations need to also maintain high levels of corporate disclosure for issues such as auditing of their supply chains, employee practices, and environmental stewardship. Often companies will use reporting frameworks such as the Global Reporting Initiative (GRI) or the Sustainability Accounting Standards Board (SASB). This practice also helps businesses improve their own processes and benchmark their performance versus their peers.

TIP

However, investors should be aware that ESG screening techniques can lead to increased exposure to large, profitable, and conservative companies, which may also result in increased exposure to certain industry, sector, or geographical biases. The bottom line is that there isn't as much historical performance data for ESG funds as there is for the broader market; therefore, researchers are still building on conclusions drawn from sustainable investing data. This has been further complicated by changing classifications or definitions for what constitutes a sustainable investment strategy over time (the previous "sin stocks" exclusion focus may be more of a "fossil fuel" exclusion focus today), making evaluation and comparisons more difficult. This leaves plenty of room for researchers to develop algorithms that optimize the portfolio's ESG profile while managing exposures to different risk factors within given limits.

TIP To keep up on ESG issues, the major financial sites do provide news and education to guide you. Check out the following:

- **Investing.com:** `www.investing.com`
- **Investopedia:** `www.investopedia.com`
- **MarketWatch:** `www.marketwatch.com`

9

Factor Investing Fundamentals

In recent years, the strategy approach of "factor investing" has been catching on, and it may be something that could boost your personal approach in the financial markets. Factor investing takes into account decades of portfolio experience and market research regarding effective approaches to portfolio management that can remove the "guesswork" about which types of securities are best able to meet a particular investor's needs.

Perhaps the simplest explanation for factors is that they can act like guard rails in your portfolio management choices. The growth in factor investing's popularity is evident in the world of portfolio management. Financial assets managed under the mantle of factor investing grew from under US$400 billion in

2013 to exceeding US$1.2 trillion in 2021. In this chapter, you find out what the appeal is.

The Definition of Factor Investing

Factor investing is an investment portfolio general strategy that favors a systematic approach utilizing factors or "shared characteristics" of individual stocks (and other assets such as bonds) that have a historical record of superior risk and return performance. These factors can range from individual characteristics such as a company's sales (revenue indicated on the company's income statement) or debt (total liabilities indicated on their balance sheet) to their performance in macro environments such as inflation or economic growth. A *factor* is a trait or characteristic that can explain the performance of a given group of stocks during various market conditions.

There are two main categories of factors:

- **Style factors** seek to identify the relevant characteristics of the individual securities (sometimes referred to as *microeconomic* traits or characteristics). Examples are the stock's volatility, market size, and valuation.

- **Macroeconomic factors** refer to the general market's environmental and economic aspects. Examples are gross domestic product (GDP) growth and inflation.

Both of these factors are covered later in this chapter.

A Brief History of Factor Investing

There have been two notable approaches that were forerunners of today's factor investing: the Capital Asset Pricing Model and the Fama and French Three-Factor Model.

The Capital Asset Pricing Model

The Capital Asset Pricing Model (CAPM) is a theory that sought to explain an asset's price performance based on how sensitive it was to the market's risks and movement. It used historical data as evidence for general market performance, as well as the performance of individual securities. Some of the findings indicated that certain key characteristics of that asset had correlation to its performance (such as price appreciation) and relative success in the general market.

Among the earliest recognized indicators was how well small stocks (small market capitalization of under C$1.5 billion) performed versus larger capitalization stocks (large-cap) during periods of economic growth.

TIP: For more details on the CAPM model, the Corporate Finance Institute is a prime resource. Check out their info here: `https://corporatefinanceinstitute.com/resources/knowledge/finance/what-is-capm-formula/`.

The Fama and French Three-Factor Model

The Fama and French Three-Factor Model (FF3FM) was constructed by the economists Eugene Fama and Kenneth French in 1992. It took CAPM (see the preceding section) and refined it further. While the CAPM model primarily focused on the market size factor, FF3FM focused on a multifactor approach and expanded that to three factors. This model became the most recognized during the early years of factor investing and was used most by some active portfolio managers of hedge funds and other large institutions, although it didn't emerge in wider usage until recent years (after 2013).

The three factors that the Fama and French Model focused on were market size, valuation, and excess return factors. A key observation with this model that also helped explain its success was that it used factors that were generally noncorrelated (meaning, more optimal diversification).

TIP: *Noncorrelated* and *correlated* are crucial concepts when looking at portfolio construction and diversification. If the assets (stocks, for example) in your portfolio are all correlated, that means that all the stocks would go up (or down) in the same market conditions, and you haven't achieved a safe and diversified portfolio. The whole point of diversification is that you have assets that perform differently in the same market events — especially if the market is correcting or declining in bearish conditions.

TIP A good explanation on this model can be found on Investopedia at `www.investopedia.com/terms/f/famaandfrenchthreefactormodel.asp`.

The Factor Categories

There are two main types of factors: style (sometimes referred to as *microeconomic*) and macroeconomic. Style factors are associated with the company (or investment vehicle) itself, while macroeconomic factors are about the company's economic environment. In both cases, the factors act as drivers for the returns (for the company's stock appreciation, for example) for that particular asset.

TIP Keep in mind that the factor categories listed here are not an exhaustive list.

Style factors

Style factors takes into account characteristics of the individual asset, such as its market size, value, industry/sector, and volatility. Style factors help explain or identify characteristics that drive the asset's price performance in the marketplace.

These factors have also been referred to as *micro-economic*, and that's a suitable description since it's a reference to the individual security or asset and what drives its performance as a singular member or participant of the overall market and economy.

Value

Looking at value typically means looking at the company's fundamentals. The *fundamentals* are the most important financial data of the company, such as the company's sales and net profits, balance sheet (assets and liabilities), and important ratios such as the price-to-earnings (P/E) ratio.

Looking at public companies (as through their common stock) through the lens of value is one of the most important factors. Value investing has survived and thrived ever since it was initially codified by the work of Benjamin Graham during the Great Depression.

TIP

Value investing is a very important discipline for those seeking a safer, long-term approach to stock investing success. Value investing strategies (and their relevant factors) should be a prime consideration for long-term investors. Keep in mind that a book you should read is the one by the acknowledged "father of value investing" Benjamin Graham's *The Intelligent Investor: The Definitive Book on Value Investing*.

One of the most important reasons to embrace value as a primary factor (especially for beginning investors) is the emphasis on stocks that are undervalued, which makes them safer than other stocks. *Undervalued* means that all the key fundamental financial aspects of the company (such as book value, the price-to-earnings ratio, and so on) generally indicate that the price of the stock is not overpriced, meaning that you won't pay an excessive stock price versus the value of the underlying company and its intrinsic worth. The reason becomes obvious in market data; overpriced stocks are more apt to decline more sharply in a correction or bear market versus reasonably priced stocks.

The bottom line is looking at the fundamentals of a stock mean a safer bet and a better chance at long-term price appreciation.

Size

The size of the asset, in this case a public company, is a reference to its market size based on market "cap" or *capitalization* (total number of shares outstanding times the price per share). The most common cap sizes used are small cap and large cap. For those seeking growth, the small-cap factor would be favored.

TIP: Large-cap assets may be safer but typically don't exhibit the same growth or price appreciation relative to the small-cap stocks. The historical data generally bears this out.

Quality

Quality is certainly joined at the hip with value. This factor should definitely among your top three considerations — especially if you're more risk-averse as a long-term investor.

Quality is a reference to the financial strength of the company. You would see this through factors such as low debt-to-asset ratios, a high return on equity, and stable earnings growth.

Dividends

Dividends are payouts to shareholders from the company. They are typically paid quarterly and are a sign of long-term financial health when the company has been paying dividends over an extended period of time (years and decades) and these dividends are paid reliably and increase over time.

TIP: Dividends should be among the prime factors considered, especially by investors who seek income and reduced risk and volatility. Dividend payouts are a tangible expression of financial strength. During times of market decline and stress, dividend-paying stocks tend to rebound well.

Additionally, the long-term market studies strongly point out that dividends over an extended period of time tend to match or exceed the rate of inflation, so this factor tends to add the bonus feature of dealing with inflation (a macroeconomic factor listed later in this chapter).

Growth

The growth factor highlights the measure of change in sales and earnings by the company in relation to its group (such as in individual industries or sectors). Is the stock growing better than its peers? If so, this factor should be considered.

As the historical market data suggests, companies with growing sales and revenue show stronger relative stock price appreciation since investors notice the growth and buy up the stock.

Volatility

Market research over an extended period of time suggests that low-volatility stocks tend to earn a better return over the long term compared to high-volatility stocks. Given that, this factor will be beneficial.

A useful indicator to look at is *beta*, which is listed at many popular financial websites for a given stock. The beta indicates how much more (or less) a given stock is volatile versus the general market (based on recent market trading data).

For beta, the stock market itself is assigned a value of 1. A stock with a beta that is less than 1 is less volatile than the general stock market, while a stock with a beta greater than 1 is more volatile than the general stock market. A stock with a beta of 1.2, for example, is considered 20 percent more volatile than the general stock market. A stock with a beta of, say, 0.9 is 10 percent less volatile than the general stock market.

A good example of a stock that has low volatility would be a large-cap public utilities company. A good example of a high-volatility stock would be a small-cap technology firm. Given these examples, an investor who is a retiree would most likely benefit from this factor to ensure getting low-volatility stocks.

Momentum

This type of factor is a better consideration for experienced investors and/or speculators seeking short-term results.

Momentum is the reference to how well the stock's price has moved upward in a given period of time (such as six months or a year) versus its peers in that particular category. Some short-term focused investors and speculators believe that if a stock is performing much better in a bullish trend, it will continue to do so in the near term. In that case, it would provide superior short-term gains versus its peers.

TIP

Although the momentum factor certainly bears this out, long-term investors should be wary. Just because a particular stock exhibits above-average upward movement that doesn't mean it will stay that way. It also doesn't mean that the stock is an appropriate selection. In the past, there have been many poor-quality stocks that have exhibited great momentum in the short term but then declined significantly.

Internet and high technology stocks exhibited powerful momentum during 1999 to 2001 but had stomach-churning declines during late 2001 to early 2002. Some went bankrupt.

Macroeconomic factors

You can compare stocks and the stock market or economy to fish in a pond. You can analyze the fish and choose great fish (using, for example, style/microeconomic factors). But you should also analyze the pond (macroeconomic factors). You could choose the greatest fish in the pond — but what if the pond is polluted? Then even the greatest fish will underperform (putting it mildly). We guess shrewd investors find a different pond.

The following sections take a look at a few major macroeconomic factors.

Economic growth

Gross domestic product (GDP) is one of the most watched economic indicators by investors and non-investors alike. It's a broad measure of the economic output (value of products and services) in a given time frame (typically a calendar quarter or year) by a nation's economy.

When GDP is growing, companies (and their stocks) are doing well. In fact, when the economy is growing and doing well, the stock market tends to outperform other markets (such as the bond market). Factors tied to economic growth such as GDP offer profitable guidance for investors.

Given that, the major investing sites regularly report this and related economic data, so this factor helps investors optimize the returns in their portfolio.

Inflation

This is a key factor especially at the time of writing (early 2022). Most folks look at price inflation (such as the rising price of consumer goods and services). However, price inflation is not a problem; it's a *symptom*. We say this because many people (including many government officials and economic policy makers unfortunately) don't understand the cause of inflation.

TIP

The cause is *monetary inflation* (the overproduction of a nation's currency supply), which precedes price inflation. When too much money is created and when that supply of money is chasing a finite basket of goods and services, the price of these goods and services will rise. The goods and services didn't become more valuable; the currency lost value (due to overproduction).

A complicating factor is the supply shortage issues during late 2021 and 2022, which augurs in cost-push inflation. When shortages occur (supply issues) and consumers contain to purchase the products in question (demand), this can further exacerbate price inflation.

In early 2021, when the money supply was increasing, this was the cue for alert investors to consider the inflation factor. This factor would have guided portfolio managers toward securities that would have outperformed in an unfolding inflationary environment.

Interest rates

Interest rates are essentially the price of borrowed money. A factor on interest rates will be key to making more optimal choices in your portfolio.

TIP

In general (and all things being equal), low interest rates are good for the economy, while high (or rising) interest rates tend to be negative. Because so much economic activity (both business and consumer activity) is tied to credit (business loans, credit cards, home mortgages, and so on), rising interest rates tend to dampen or diminish economic activity, while low or decreasing rates tend to do the opposite.

Given that, factors tied to interest rates will help you avoid stocks (and bonds) that would be harmed by rising interest rates so your portfolio can continue to perform satisfactorily.

An Example of a Factor-Based Portfolio

Consider a simple example of how a factor-based portfolio may differ from a traditional, non-factor-based approach.

For decades, one of the simplest portfolio constructions was 60 percent stocks and 40 percent bonds. After that simple diversification of two different asset classes, there may be diversification within each asset class.

The stock portion may have a mix of large-cap stocks, mid-cap stocks, and small-cap stocks. The bonds may be a mix of investment-grade corporate bonds.

The factor-based approach would make portfolio choices based on investment characteristics that have performed better than a random mix of securities. The stocks would be selected based on style factors such as value and quality so selections are more optimal given the general market conditions at that time. If the general market were experiencing inflation, inflation factors would be used to select stocks that perform better than average in an inflationary environment. The inflation factor is a macroeconomic factor described earlier in this chapter.

The bonds portion of the portfolio would also be viewed through the prism of appropriate factors. If the investor or client were seeking safety, for example, low-risk factors such as short bond maturities and high bond ratings would be used to limit market risk.

The Upside and Downside of Factor Investing

Diversification is a rock-solid never-ending part of the foundation of successful investing (especially stock investing). Choosing the stocks of financially sound public companies (that had "good fundamentals") that are diversified among different industries is an important long-term consideration. Factor investing helps take this approach to a more effective level by reducing risk and enhancing returns.

Factor investing may sound attractive since it has so much weight behind it from academic studies and market data research, but it's far from perfect. Not all factors can work well consistently — the market can change quickly and make one factor turn from a positive to a negative.

Say, for example, you embrace the size factor in your approach. This factor puts a lot of emphasis on small-cap stocks, which may work well during a robust bull market, but you could get hammered during an unfolding bear market.

On the other hand, if you choose an approach that works well during a bear market, that leaves your portfolio underperforming during bullish times. The value investing factor, for example, may work out fine during a bear market or a sideways market, but it won't be optimal during a roaring bull market when value stocks lag the performance of growth-oriented choices.

TIP

Have a mix of factors working for you. Just as diversification works well with different asset classes in your overall portfolio, a mix of factors will work out better long-term versus too much reliance on a single factor approach. A portfolio approach with a single factor will make you look like a genius if that factor is shining bright — but you'll see negative returns if that factor is (temporarily) out of favor with current market conditions.

Factor Investing through ETFs and Mutual Funds

For some folks, dealing with constructing a portfolio with an optimal balance of factors may seem daunting — but no worries! You can get a factor investing strategy put in place with a few mouse clicks by choosing funds that adhere to factors. There are exchange-traded funds (ETFs; see Chapter 2) and mutual funds that have emerged in recent years that can make it convenient to do a factor-based approach.

TIP

To find ETFs, do a search for factor investing at the ETF database site (`www.etfdb.com`). For mutual funds, do a similar search at `www.mutualfunds.com`. You can find Canadian assets at both sites.

About the Authors

Brendan Bradley is currently nonexecutive chairman (Fregnan and iPushPull) on the advisory board (FINTECH Circle, HUBX, Limeglass, RISE Financial Technologies, and Waymark Tech) for many early-stage FinTech firms, as well as cofounder of Seismic Foundry, a seed-stage venture capital group. He is the coauthor of *FinTech For Dummies.*

Susanne Chishti is the CEO and founder of FINTECH Circle, the leading global FinTech community focused on FinTech investments and corporate innovation strategies, and founder of the FINTECH Circle Institute, a FinTech learning platform offering innovation workshops to C-level executives and FinTech courses. She is the coauthor of *FinTech For Dummies.*

Kiana Danial is an award-winning, internationally recognized personal investing and wealth management expert. She's a highly sought-after professional speaker, author, and executive coach who delivers workshops and seminars to corporations, universities, and investment groups. She is the author of *Cryptocurrency Investing For Dummies.*

Steve Gormley is a renowned expert in the legal marijuana sector, with nearly 30 years' experience developing, branding, marketing, launching, managing, and operating businesses in the U.S. and international markets. He is widely considered a pioneer in the cannabis industry, with nearly a decade of professional experience in the sector. He is the author of *Investing in Cannabis For Dummies.*

James Jockle is CMO and executive vice president, Global Marketing & Corporate Communications for Numerix. He is the coauthor of *FinTech For Dummies.*

Peter Kent and **Tyler Bain** are the coauthors of *Bitcoin For Dummies.* For decades, Peter has been explaining complicated technical subjects to regular people; he knows how to explain technology in a way that you can understand. He's the author of around 60 technology books. Tyler has been in the cryptocurrency mining trenches gaining experience in the ecosystem for a few years. He is also a professional engineer registered in the state of Colorado and studied engineering with an electrical specialty at the Colorado School of Mines.

Matt Krantz is a financial journalist who specializes in investing topics and personal finance and is the management editor for *Investor's Business Daily.* In addition to writing for *IBD,* his work has appeared in *USA Today* and *Money* magazine. He has covered financial markets and Wall Street for decades, concentrating on developments affecting individual investors and their portfolios. He is the author of *Online Investing For Dummies.*

Tiana Laurence (T) and **Seoyoung Kim (Soy)** have been friends for years and are excited to write their first book together as The Investor and The Professor. T and Soy both love food, wine, and interesting conversations, and this book has materialized at the intersection of their shared interests.

James Maendel is the founder of Maendel Wealth, an investment advisory firm. He is one of the first investment advisors to earn the Certificate in Blockchain and Digital Assets from the New York Institute of Finance (DACFP/RIADAC). He is the coauthor of *Factor Investing For Dummies.*

Paul Mladjenovic is a national speaker, educator, and author. He was a Certified Financial Planner (CFP) from 1985 to 2021. Since 1981, he has specialized in investing, financial planning, and entrepreneurship issues. He has done over 2,500 seminars, workshops, and lectures since 1983. Paul is the author of *Stock Investing For Dummies* and *High-Level Investing For Dummies,* and the coauthor of *Factor Investing For Dummies.*

Steven R. O'Hanlon is the CEO and president of Numerix, the leading FinTech provider of innovative capital markets technology solutions and real-time intelligence applications for trading and risk management. He is the coauthor of *FinTech For Dummies.*

Dawn Patrick is both the COO and executive vice president of Global Operations for Numerix, the leading provider of innovative capital markets technology solutions and real-time intelligence applications for trading and risk management. She is the coauthor of *FinTech For Dummies.*

Russell Wild has been a fee-only (takes no commissions) financial advisor for the past 20 years. He heads Global Portfolios, LLC, an investment advisory firm based in Philadelphia, Pennsylvania. He is the author of *Exchange-Traded Funds For Dummies.*

